In "I Made It!" author Juana M. Ortiz chronicles her life from a childhood in the Dominican Republic to a multiple-degree holding author in the U.S. As with any memoir, Ortiz highlights the difficulties and obstacles she faced on her way to achieving her primary goal of becoming educated and self-sufficient. In addition to being an immigrant, Ortiz copes with cerebral palsy and the impact that has on her life. Despite the issues caused by the CP and language barriers, Ortiz steadfastly pursues education and self-reliancy without resorting to pity or blaming others.

The education system in particular was not yet set up to handle the difficulties Ortiz had. She recognizes her own difficulties and finds ways to surpass them by putting aside more time to work, seeking out amenable professors, and just continuing to work hard. Spoiler alert, this inspirational tale ends with Ortiz educated, self-reliant, and eager to help others as much as she can.

"I Made It!" is more of an inspirational story than a memoir. Ortiz uses her experiences with CP and as an immigrant to highlight the underlying drive that everyone shares. A desire to improve themselves, make something out of their lives, and hopefully help others achieve those same goals. Ortiz shines through her writing and her dogged determination an upbeat personality pours out of every word. The story is engaging and tempered with both humor and sadness. Obstacles rise up to meet her, and sometimes they knock her back a few paces, but she refuses to let anything stop her. Her loving family, trusted professors, and colleagues all seem to pop up just when Ortiz needs a little push not to give up, but the ultimate drive belongs to her and her alone.

This is a story that anyone can sympathize and connect with. Ortiz wants readers to see her, and others with disabilities, as human beings with just as much will to thrive as anyone else. With the help of mentors, disability advocacy groups, and her own powerful self-drive, Ortiz steps up and works hard for what she wants. At the end of the day, that is something most readers will resonate with emotionally. "I Made It!" is well-written, simply told, and full of heart and pearls of wisdom. It not only holds CP up to the light, but the life of an immigrant, a student, a daughter, and a woman seeking more out of life despite the barriers thrown up against her.

Reviewer: John Murray
Rating: 5 Star Review
Pacific Book Review

"I have to accept myself in order for others to accept Juana."

Juana Ortiz was born with cerebral palsy in the Dominican Republic (DR) in 1972. The DR was a poor country with little medical care for a child medical authorities gave little hope of recovery and even less for living a productive life. Prejudices and lack of awareness and resources created what could have been a hopeless situation for the first child of young parents. But voices filled with bleakness wouldn't be accepted by the extended Ortiz family. They vowed to see Juana survive physically and mentally. This is Juana's firsthand account of their love and her resilience.

Life for Juana wasn't much better when she first moved to the United States at the age of fifteen. But though she struggled with the learning process, her mother and father embraced her drive for being enrolled in a public school although older than others, attending high school, and being accepted into college. Despite having all odds against her, she persevered. In college a professor recognized that her greatest talent is found in her ability to write creatively. A new world opened up for Juana, where she shared her joys, fears, triumphs, and successes in a voice that can only belong to this remarkable young woman. Her physical challenges became second, as she revealed how positive she had become.

She isn't afraid to "get real" when sharing how this disability impacts both hers, as well as her family's, daily life. But her accomplishments prove that we can all learn to fly, even if we have broken wings. Juana dedicates the book to her parents who were so deserving of this honor. Readers may also add the inescapable value of mentors who reached out with hands and hearts in order for her to achieve her goals.

Barbara Mims Deming
US Review of Books

I Made it!

Juana M. Ortiz

authorHOUSE®

AuthorHouse™
1663 Liberty Drive
Bloomington, IN 47403
www.authorhouse.com
Phone: 1 (800) 839-8640

Published by AuthorHouse   12/12/2016

ISBN: 978-1-5049-0164-2 (sc)
ISBN: 978-1-5049-0163-5 (e)

Library of Congress Control Number: 2015904530

Print information available on the last page.

Any people depicted in stock imagery provided by Thinkstock are models, and such images are being used for illustrative purposes only. Certain stock imagery © Thinkstock.

This book is printed on acid-free paper.

Because of the dynamic nature of the Internet, any web addresses or links contained in this book may have changed since publication and may no longer be valid. The views expressed in this work are solely those of the author and do not necessarily reflect the views of the publisher, and the publisher hereby disclaims any responsibility for them.

CONTENTS

Optimism is the faith that leads to achievement. Nothing can be done without hope and confidence.

Helen Keller

To Mom & Dad
Dedicado A Mis Padres

INTRODUCTION

As a child and all the way through my early 30s, I kept everything to myself. I used to wear an invisible mask, pretending that I was OK. I didn't have the courage to sit down with my family and tell them how I really felt about living with a disability.

I am from the Dominican Republic (DR), a country where prejudice against people with disabilities is strong. I was born with cerebral palsy (CP), a condition that affected me physically. Back in the 70s and the 80s there was not much information about this condition. Despite my family's financial hardship and the lack of awareness and resources about CP, my parents did everything possible to help me have a good quality of life.

Having gone through tough situations since my childhood, I decided to share these experiences with my readers for three major reasons. First, writing about my struggles has helped me to cope with so many wounds from the past. It has been therapeutic to open up and let others know what happened, how I felt about it, and how these life events have helped me to grow as a person. Second, I want to show how I made it. I set goals most people thought I could not achieve, but I did, and I want others to know they can, too.

Third, since there still a lot of misunderstanding about people with disabilities and their education. I want to advocate for the inclusion of students with disabilities in mainstream classes all the way through college.

From the time I was a little girl, one of the hardest things that I had to deal with was the limitation imposed by society on people with disabilities. Since childhood, I was labeled as a person incapable of carrying out simple activities, such as attending school. This is mostly due to lack of awareness, and I aimed to change perceptions whenever I could

Even though I grew up surrounded by the love and the support of my family, I had to deal with plenty of prejudice. Back in the DR just by walking outside, I suffered the cruelty of other children who ridiculed me. Sometimes adults could be equally hurtful.

Even after I arrived in the United States (US), I was stereotyped because of my disability. In the winter of 1988, when I was 15, my family moved to Paterson, New Jersey. When I arrived and saw snow on the ground, I knew my way of life would be very different from how it had been back in the DR. Cold yet beautiful, the snow on the ground symbolized both the new obstacles and opportunities that lay ahead in my new country.

It all started with my expectation of attending school for the first time. I was in the US. This was the land of opportunity, where students with disabilities had the chance to attend school. At least, that's what I heard back in the DR from my relatives who were already living in the US.

Since I couldn't attend school down there, I saw my chance of becoming educated in America as a great privilege. However, it took me a while to experience the joy of being in school. Before I could attend, I had to go through a process that took several months and much help from others. It was all new to my mother and me. We did not speak English, and I had no idea what was going on. All I knew was that soon I would attend classes, just as most other American children do.

By the time I started school I was already 16, a crucial age for any teenager. Getting used to a new culture, a new language, a different climate, and the prospect of attending school for the first time would have been a challenge for anyone, let alone a teenager.

In the process of trying to enroll in school, I discovered that the definition of "learning" turned out to be something different from what I thought it should be. To the system, I was not seen as a student capable of fitting into a mainstream classroom. Due to my CP I was enrolled in special education. Lessons like math, English and science were often not taught in special ed classes. Yet once I started classes, despite my lack of education in the past and unfamiliarity with English, I was exceeding all expectations. But within the school nobody seemed to notice or at least they didn't show any signs of noticing.

However, outside of the school's environment, my ability and my desire to learn things beyond independent living skills became visible to others. In fall 1993, I became one of the first students with CP in the city of Paterson to be included in a regular high school. Due to my physical limitations, my age, my ethnicity, and my lack of education, new challenges emerged. Through that period. I wasn't the typical student. And, my goal of getting an education didn't end with a high school diploma.

I enrolled in college and attended from my late 20s through my early 30s, an experience that put me through some tough periods. My major goal was to obtain a college degree, but academically I wasn't doing well. Plus, I was discouraged by several people who simply assumed that I could not succeed in college. I lost hope. I didn't see any improvement in my grades and felt disappointed.

All my expectations for the future had been based on earning a college degree, but suddenly that dream seemed to vanish. My journey became a road full of bumps that I didn't know how to navigate. I was on my own. I saw myself as a loser. My life didn't have meaning anymore.

I had lost faith in myself and didn't trust people anymore. I was desperately searching for a purpose to keep going. Then one day, in an unexpected way, I found the purpose that I was looking for. Some might call it coincidence or destiny. I called it God's miracle, a purpose to not give up.

CHAPTER 1

CEREBRAL PALSY

During labor, my mother didn't receive medical care on time. My brain failed to get adequate oxygen and by the time I was born, the left side of my body had already been affected. Consequently, I developed cerebral palsy (CP), which affects my body movements, postures, and muscles. It affects the way that I walk, stand, and talk.

I was born August 15, 1972, and according to the doctor, the expectation for my recovery was poor. Despite the dire predictions, my parents didn't give up. My family lived in the Dominican Republic (DR), a poor country, with few resources and little information about CP. Mami and Papi didn't deny what was going on with me and, with the support of our family, they decided to carry on.

I was my parents' first-born child. Mami was in her early 20s and Papi was in his mid-20s. They were very young and their financial situation was weak, but they did not let that stop them from doing their best for me.

My parents started researching resources to get help for me. They were able to obtain information about options available in Santo Domingo, the capital city of DR. Papi used to work as a cab driver, driving a car back and forth from Bani, where we lived, to Santo Domingo, so he was familiar with the city. Bani was a small town located toward the south of the DR.

Starting from the time I was six months old, Papi, Mami, and I drove to the only rehabilitation center that existed in the area at the time. My parents had to pay for the services. Papi was the sole wage earner of the family and Mami was a stay-at-home mom. Papi didn't make a lot of money, but my parents managed to pay the medical bills and the costs of the medication and special shoes I needed. When my parents couldn't afford to pay for something, Papi's parents helped with the expenses.

All the things a baby starts doing at a certain age, I started to do later, such as eating on my own, getting dressed, and using the bathroom. Each of these accomplishments was a long process for me, but I succeeded, thanks to the perseverance and efforts of my parents and of Papi's mother, Carlita,

I needed to have physical, occupational, and speech therapy to have a better quality of life. I didn't start walking until age three, which was a big achievement due to my condition and lack of resources. From the age of six months until I was nine or ten years old, I received professional health care including regular checkups by doctors, speech therapy, and physical therapy. Some therapy sessions were at the rehabilitation center, but others were at home. Mami also received some training in order to give me therapy at home. This was the key to my progress, along with the support from the health care professionals.

At home, Mami was also in charge of the prescription medications I took daily. One of them was Valium, which helped me to stay calm. During my childhood I had periods when I became very agitated, sometimes over minor things. If one of my brothers tried to take a toy away from me, instead of asking him to give it back, I would scratch his face or throw at him anything that I had in my hands. As a result, Mami kept her eyes on my nails and when they grew too long, she cut them. Fortunately, nothing serious ever happened.

Papi often helped Mami with my daily physical therapy, because I needed two people to assist me. Sometimes Mami's sister Soris, who lived with us, would be Mami's helper. While I was lying on the table in the living room, one person was stretching my left leg while the other person held my right leg down. This continued for different exercises. I didn't feel any pain from the therapy, but I did feel uncomfortable, because the stretches were to loosen the tightness of the tendons in my legs.

By age nine, I could do some of the occupational therapy on my own. I had a jar full of small stones. Once a day, I grabbed the jar, emptied all the stones on the floor, and with my weak hand, I picked up each stone and put it back in the jar. It was a real challenge for me to pick up the stones.

My at-home therapy was a blend of modern medicine and traditional treatments. My Abuela (grandmother) didn't have a degree in the health field, but she knew a lot about homemade remedies. She made a treatment with cooking oil to put on my knees in order to help relax my tendons. I sat on the floor and Abuela spread greasy oil all over my knees, using a feather from the domestic chicken that my grandparents raised in their backyard. That treatment helped, too.

I was the oldest of three children and the only girl. Despite my disability, I was raised the same way as my brothers. I was four years older than Alfredo and six years older than Benito. I got no special treatment. If I did something wrong I was punished. My parents' friends used to tell them that I should not be punished, but my parents didn't listen. One day, when I was about eight years old and was losing my teeth, I was arguing with Mami. She told me to be quiet and to stop arguing, but I didn't pay any attention. Then she slapped my face and my tooth fell out. That was a big lesson for me as a child. Listen while an adult is talking.

I consider myself to be lucky. Papi has always given all his support to Mami, and he has never blamed her for what happened to me at birth. I had heard of marriages that broke apart when the father blamed the mother if their child had a disability or when the father rejected the idea of having a child with a disability, not unusual in Hispanic culture. In some cases, it is the mother who refuses to accept the situation, and sometimes, an entire family is embarrassed by having a family member with a disability. They may believe that the child's disability is punishment for something one of them did in the past.

The society in which we were living was cruel and unjust toward children with disabilities and their families. People pitied us and treated my parents as though their daughter came to them damaged, the way a piece of furniture might be delivered broken. So besides of having a child with CP, my parents had to deal with the ignorance of others. This was discouraging for them, yet they never made me feel I was to blame for anything. I consider myself privileged, because I had support not only from my parents, but also from the rest of my family, too.

Society

Childhood & Homeschooling

I was just ten years old. Every weekday morning I stood by the door of the backyard looking at the narrow street of Las Mercedes in Bani. Quietly, I observed the other kids passing by wearing their school uniforms. Sometimes they wore a yellow shirt or a blue one with light brown pants. They carried books in their arms on their way to school. I wanted to go to school with them, but I had to stay home with Mami, instead.

One day, my mother told me that I couldn't attend school because of my physical limitation. That was a key moment, because I became aware that I was different from the other kids, not just physically, but also from a sociological point of view. Even when my parents wanted me to attend school, the school system wasn't prepared to deal with a student who had a weird body mold. I didn't know any other children who had CP. None of the children in my family or in my neighborhood walked or talked the way that I did. My physical appearance was unique. When I was outside, people stared at me because of the way I walked.

My body didn't have straight lines; they were curled. My feet seemed impossible to lift up from the floor as people normally do when walking. My mouth was always open, like the letter "U." When I talked, I sounded drunk, even though I was not. To most people, I was an alien, like someone from another planet. Other children made fun of me because of the way I walked and talked. I tried to ignore them and pretend that it didn't bother me, even though it did. I often heard people say that I was not a normal being.

Home was my cage, though I wasn't forced to stay inside. My brothers and Soris who was more like my older sister than my aunt, left for school at 7:30 in the morning. Papi went to work and Mami took care of the house. Every member of my family had some type of responsibility: attend school, go to work, take care of the house. Their daily routines were full, without much free time.

My daily schedule was empty. There were no major events written in my calendar. As a result, I became a designer, filling every empty spot by watering the plants, doing some dishes, and playing by myself. There was not much that I could do.

My father's parents lived next door, and I spent the days going back and forth between both houses. Abuela, my father's mother, was influential in the way that I was raised. She was very traditional in terms of gender roles. Because I was a girl, she thought it was important for me to do housework. I learned about gender roles early in life.

In my culture, a female should learn how to cook, wash the clothes, and clean the house, among other household duties. I helped Abuela do the dishes, water the plants, and sweep the backyard. Then, I spent the rest of the day playing games, listening to the radio, and watching TV. In the backyard, I looked at the sky where birds flew by over the house. In my imagination, I flew with them. This was my only way to leave home for the day.

Even though I didn't attend formal school while I was growing up, I learned how to read and write. First, I attended homeschooling, but it was a little different from what homeschooling means to most people. The sessions didn't take place at my house; but at the teacher's home, instead. Ms. Mariana, was a woman in her mid-sixties who ran a small school at her house, which we called escuelita.

I attended escuelita for a couple of years. There were around fifteen students about my age in the class, which took place in the teacher's backyard, a few blocks from my home. The class sessions ran for a couple of hours in the afternoon, Mondays through Fridays. Ms. Mariana taught basic lessons: reading, writing and math. I did all the assignments on my own and felt a sense of belonging to the class, except when it was time for us to take a break. All the kids got up and started playing. At that moment, I became an alien again.

I remained sitting in my chair, like an outsider, while my classmates played. I avoided playing to prevent falling and hurting myself, but another reason I did not join in the play was my fear that I would not be welcome. That may have been true, because nobody else encouraged me to join in, either. I wanted to be let out of the box, but aliens are never asked to join the human race.

Besides going to the escuelita, I was also taught at home by my parents and my father's younger brother. My uncle worked as a teacher in a private Catholic school where he asked if there was a possibility for me to attend, but the administrators there refused me. My physical appearance was a strange phenomenon to the staff. Never before they had seen such a creature. They didn't have the right tools to deal with me, because there wasn't much information available about my condition. Also the school wasn't structurally accessible.

Despite all the obstacles I faced at a young age, regarding becoming educated, I had an enormous desire to learn. Not being able to attend school didn't stop me from learning. I was self-motivated and wanted to keep learning regardless of the circumstances. There was a voice inside me repeating over and over, "I have to learn." So I became my own tutor. I borrowed my brothers' books from grammar school and started reading them.

I loved learning about the natural and social sciences. By the time I was about 12 years old, I was reading newspapers. I always saw Papi and Abuelo, my father's father, reading newspapers. I also saw Mami reading short novels. Those newspapers and "novelitas" were all an attraction for me. Their content, titles, images and colors lit up my intellectual curiosity.

For a couple of years, Mami ran a small store from home, which was typical for women in the DR. That allowed her to make some money while still taking care of the house. In other words, Mami was able to balance her role as a mom and as business owner. Our living room was large, so Mami divided it into two sections, and used one side of the room as the store.

The name of the store "Fantasia Maritza," included my middle name, Maritza. In the DR, people are often called by their middle name rather than the first name. When I saw my name on the sign, I felt I was part of a major retail store. The customers who walked into the store or just passed by saw my name, "Fantasia Maritza." They didn't see an alien.

I helped out in the store in the mornings, because that was when Mami needed the most help. She sold clothing, mostly women's underwear, stockings, and linens for the bed.

Mami was a storekeeper, but she was still the woman of the house and had to make lunch for the family. She usually cooked rice, beans and meat. When a customer entered the store, I notified Mami, who was in the kitchen. After the customers left, she went back to cooking. Lunch was served at noon. By that time my brothers and Soris were back from school. Sometimes Papi took a break from his bus driver job and stopped by for lunch too.

Lunch was the main meal of the day throughout the community. Since nobody was in the streets during lunch time, Mami closed the store from noon to 2:00 p.m. The store hours were 8:00 a.m. to 12 noon and 2:00 p.m. to 6:00 p.m., Monday through Saturday.

At early age, I had to deal with a lot prejudice. As a child I didn't understand why I was treated unfairly by others. Sometimes when I went to bed I asked myself, "Why do I have CP? Why I can't go to school? Why I can't play like the rest of the kids?" I saw them jumping and running.

Even though Mami had told me the reason why before, her explanation wasn't enough. I didn't understand why I had CP and the other kids did not. At night, as I lay down to sleep, my pillow got wet with my tears. The next morning, I would wake up pretending that nothing happened. I was afraid of asking questions, because I didn't want my family to feel sorry. I already had enough with the way I was treated by society.

Teen Years

The big date was fast approaching. In two more years I would be turning 15, a significant age for a girl in Hispanic culture. Very slowly my childhood was slipping into the past. Soon I would become a señorita. No more playing with dolls. Despite the changes that my body started to experience, I would not be like the rest of the señoritas from my town.

The other girls my age had an active lifestyle. They attended high schools and had friends. Las señoritas go out in groups to the movie, to the clubs, and even for a walk to the park. They also have overnights at their friends' homes. They have *enamorados* too, guys that flirt with them. At 9:30 a.m. on their day off from school, I see las señoritas pass by my house on their way back from the *colmado,* (grocery store). They were doing *mandados* (errands) for their mothers. They carried brown bags full of rice, oil, beans, onion and pepper. A little earlier they went to the mercado (market) to buy fresh meat for *la comida (*lunch) the heavy meal of the day.

Las señoritas wore ponytails, shorts, some make-up, and T-shirts showing their belly. The sun, along with the warm temperature, made their brown skin gleam as las señoritas swung their hips when they walked. They sang aloud to the hottest pop songs at the time. Across the street were *los pretendientes* (guys who hope to become a girl's boyfriend or husband) who flirted with the girls., *"Mamacita que buena estas,"* "You, hot." They blew kisses to las señoritas. The girls kept walking and tried to ignore the guys.

I didn't walk to the stores. I didn't wear shorts. I just wore skirts or dresses to cover my knees. None of the boys blew kisses to me. My hips didn't move the same way as the hips of las señoritas.

Once the señoritas from next-door arrived home, they started helping their mothers with heavy housework. These girls cleaned the house, mopped the floor, and washed clothes by hand for their parents and the younger children. They also cooked lunch. Since they were señoritas, they must share housework and show their parents that when the time came to be married, they were ready to meet the expectations imposed by society on their gender: To take care of their house and kids, and be a good partner to their husbands.

I didn't meet any of those expectations. I didn't have any friends to go out with. I didn't go to school. I didn't walk by myself to the grocery stores. I didn't carry heavy bags of food items. I didn't cook heavy meals for my family. I didn't mop the floor. I didn't wash the clothes by hand. I didn't meet any of the expectations society has for young women. I was different.

In those days, stereotypes were still strong in the DR. There was the perception that people with disabilities were worthless. Each time I walked along the streets people asked my parents what was wrong with me. *¿Ella Hablá? ¿Ella entiende cuando le hablán? Que pena? (*Does she talk? Does she understand what others are saying to her? Poor thing.) I disliked hearing the same questions and expressions of pity over and over again.

Even though my family treated me with love and respect, society pushed me to the side because I was different. Besides dealing with the same issues that most teens had to deal with in terms of identity and physical changes, I also had to deal with physical limitations and social rejection due to the CP.

As a teenager in my town I never fit in, a circumstance that started in my childhood. When I was a little girl, I didn't have the opportunity to attend school. Special education didn't exist in the country back then. Even though I wanted to attend school, I couldn't. All this turmoil from childhood was quietly building up inside of me. Once I reached the teen years, I became even more aware of the prejudice toward people with disabilities.

I was 13 years old, when my life started to go down a dark road. I had no idea where to turn. Should I go right or left? I felt hopeless. Depression set in. I didn't know what to expect in the future. I had no idea how my life would be once I reached adulthood. The main role for a female was to marry, have kids, and take care of a partner. These goals were unreachable for me. I didn't meet the criteria. In my depressed state, I was focused on everything that I couldn't accomplish.

Mami was very concerned about my emotional well-being. One day I heard her talking on the phone with Papi, telling him her worries regarding my emotional state. Papi had moved to New York City to find work, due to the financial hardship in the DR. Papi asked Mami to put me on the phone. Papi told me to take care of myself and to try to do something that I enjoyed. Hearing Mami tell Papi her concerns for me, and hearing Papi trying to console me reminded me of how much I was loved by my parents. That made a huge difference. I felt worth something as a person.

Life had meaning. The dark road of my teen years started to get brighter each day.

After my conversation with Papi, Mami and Soris motivated me to get busy, so I would have something to do, since I was home all day. I helped out more around the house, swept the backyard, and just became more active at home. Becoming aware of how much I was loved by my family and that I had worth as a person, helped me to recover from depression.

The biggest day of my teen years finally arrived. On August 15, 1987 I turned fifteen years old. I was now a señorita. I didn't have the big quinceañera birthday party, traditional in Hispanic cultures. I wished for one, the way that I saw it in the telenovelas soap-operas. Usually the parents host a big party for the quinceañera, inviting relatives and friends. The night of the party, the quinceañera wears a pink or white long gown and a crown. She dances with her father to the traditional quinceañera song, "El Vals De la Mariposa." (Butterfly Waltz)

Even though my parents didn't host a quinceañera party for me I had a nice fifteenth birthday, which I will always remember. This was the first time that I got so many birthday gifts. Soris bought me a pink and a white cake decorated with a small pink flower on the top. Tio Arcenio, Papi's younger brother, gave me a black and white teddy bear.

My parents bought me a nice bouquet of yellow, red, and white flowers. Mami made me a pink outfit. Pink symbolized being a female, but also being a girl who is turning into a woman. That day, Papi called me from New York to wish me a happy birthday.

Soris lived with us since before I turned five. Before then, she lived with my grandparents in the countryside, Rioarriba, but her school was located in Bani. Though Bani is now a major city in the province of Peravia, back then it was a small town surrounded by farmland. Since Soris would have a long commute to school from Rioarriba, she ended up living with us. She was a only few years older than I was and acted like a big sister, watching over my two younger brothers and me. She was a big help for Mami, since I needed a lot of care and assistance with eating, getting dressed, and other ordinary activities.

As I got older, I gave Soris a hard time, because I became jealous of the relationship between her and Mami. Since Soris was older, Mami had more mature conversations with her than with me. They even shared some secrets that I was not allowed to know about due to my age.

At home, everybody shared the same radio because that was all my parents could afford. It was a small red and gray radio that ran on batteries. Sometimes when Soris turned on the radio and chose a certain station, I would sneak up and try to change the station. I would do the same thing when Soris was watching a certain program on our black and white TV. I would try to change the channel. Now I admit that I was being mean to someone who cared for me. Maybe I was acting out because of my disability and the way people treated me. I am not excusing myself, but I this was my way of letting out all the hurt that I kept inside.

Papi Leaves the DR for the USA

I knew Papi was leaving for New York because the financial situation in the DR was getting tougher. His job as a bus driver was not bringing in enough money to support the family. He was the only one working and even though Mami was still running the small store, that was not enough. Papi left when I was 11 years old, Alfredo was seven, and Benito was only five. I remember seeing Mami sitting in her chair, reading the letters from Papi, while tears ran down her cheeks.

She missed Papi very much, but at the same time, she had to be strong for the family. For four years there was no man to paint the house at Christmas, to move the furniture so Mami could clean behind it, or to carry the heavy bags from the grocery store. There was no man to drive us to Mami's parents, when we went to visit once or twice at a month. They lived in the countryside, a few miles from our home.

Before Mami went to bed, she made sure the door was locked, because there was no man to watch over us, and everybody in the neighborhood knew that. When she had to go to the bank or to the store to run her errands, she had to be careful of appearances. If she was seen talking or walking with another man, rumors could start that she was seeing somebody behind Papi's back.

Papi called home two or three times a month and once in a while, he wrote Mami letters. At that time, there was no Internet, Skype, Was'up or any of the other technology that exists today to help people stay in touch. Mami was the one who talked the most with Papi when he called. My brothers and I talked to him briefly, mostly to ask for his blessings, which is a cultural ritual. Mami would send Papi photos of the three of us, so he could see how big we were getting.

At 11 years old, I had fresh memories about Papi in the DR. I thought about when he came home from work and how, after dinner, the six of us, my parents, my brothers, Soris, and I would sit in the living room to watch local TV shows or American programs translated into Spanish. Papi sat in the rocking chair, holding Benito in his arms and rocking him to sleep.

Other evenings, Papi read the newspaper after dinner, then went to his parents' house next door for a visit and some conversation. On Sunday mornings he sometimes went to play softball with a group of friends and took my brothers with him. I was upset, because I wanted to go, too. Mami explained to me that the event was for boys only, not girls, and that's why I couldn't go.

Not having my father physically present made home feel empty, especially at times like Christmas, Father's Day, and when one of us got sick. Would I ever see Papi again? I asked myself that question many times during those years.

CHAPTER 2

FROM THE DOMINICAN REPUBLIC TO PATERSON, NEW JERSEY

On a cold January night in 1988, Mami, my brothers and I moved to the United States. We went to live in Paterson, New Jersey where Papi and Mami's parents, Gregoria and Pedro, were already living.

Before we arrived from the airport, Mami's mother, Abuela Gregoria, cooked us a welcoming meal of rice and black beans. When we all sat to eat, the way of serving was the traditional Dominican way, women serving the men first and then the children. Abuela served Abuelo Pedro, Mami's father. He was sitting at the table with Papi. Mami served him and then served the three of us children.

I was seated at the table next to my brothers who were sitting on milk crates used as chairs. It was the first time I saw black beans mixed with rice. I thought they looked like yuck and said to myself, *"Necesitaré ir al baño después de que yo coma eso."*(I will need to go to the bathroom after I eat that).

On my second night in Paterson, I experienced a kind of miracle. Mami was standing by the window in the living room. Suddenly, I heard her voice, *"Juana ven para que veas algo"*—"Juana, come see something."

I approached the window and I saw white dots falling to the ground. It was my first time seeing the city change into white. The next morning, I was amazed at the sunshine after the storm the night before. This was a new episode in my life. I had the chance to observe the power of Mother Nature from another place on the planet.

The snow was a unique experience for me. It was different from what I had thought it would be. I enjoyed watching as everything turned to white. In the past, I had heard people talking about snow or white Christmas, but being able to see it or feel it in my body as it was snowing was even more exciting,

Back in the DR the image that I had of the winter season was the Christmas tree that Mami made using white toilet paper. She used to decorate the tree with Christmas lights and cover the tree branches with little pieces of white paper in each of the small hollows.

Watching the real snow falling, I could see how a busy, loud city could be magically transformed into a place of beauty and peace. I did not know yet how much I would be transformed by my life in this new country.

Balancing Two Cultures: Remembering My Former Life

Pedro Mir's poem, *Hay Un Pais En El Mundo* (There is One Country in the World) brings me back to my childhood in Bani where I can feel the sunshine warming my back and the soft breezes caressing my face on hot afternoons. As I read the poem, I inhaled the aroma of roasting coffee mixed with the fragrance of the wet ground. I heard the early morning music of raindrops and rooster songs.

I pictured the games I used to play with my brothers in the backyard. Sometimes we played "hide and seek." One of us would hide behind the door in the living room, then the other two would look for him…or her if I was the one behind the door. We had fun making up our own games, too. We loved arranging the chairs in a line and taking a seat on our imaginary train to faraway places.

One of the most exciting days for a child in our culture is, January 6, *El dia de Los Tres Reyes Magos* (The Three Kings Day), honoring the Magi who brought gifts to the infant Christ child. It was our tradition that the Three Kings, not Santa Claus, brought gifts to children on this holiday. On the night of January 5, I would go to bed early in order for the Kings to come and place gifts next to my pillow.

The next morning I woke up early, thrilled to open my gifts. Though I didn't receive a dozen presents. I was delighted with my dolls, coffee-tea set, new skirt, and pretty blouse. January 6 was always a happy, exciting day.

My Life in Paterson

Soon after moving to Paterson, at age 15, I realized my life would not be the same. For the first time I had to wear a coat. I couldn't wear short skirts or sandals until summer. There was no backyard where I could go out to sit and look at the blue sky and daydream. All these things that were once part of my daily life were replaced by the sidewalks, car horns, and busy pace of city life. I reminded myself that I was no longer in the DR, but it was not easy to adapt to living in a place where my way of life had changed so much.

For the first time, I felt like a stranger in a place where everything was unfamiliar. It was like being born again, and all the things that I lived through before were no longer part of my new surroundings.

Back in the DR, I never thought I would end up wearing second-hand clothes in America. When my family and I first arrived in Paterson, Papi bought us winter clothes. He worked as a cab driver in the Bronx, New York, and didn't have enough money to buy us new clothes. He had already spent money on the immigration paper work, the airfare, and the rent for the house that we moved into. The best option was to buy second-hand clothes since it was cheaper.

The day after the storm, Papi drove Mami, my brothers and me to New York City to visit Papi's older brother, Leonel, at the bodega he owned. Leonel had lived in New York for many years. For the first time, I saw tall buildings, trains, a lot with cars parked one behind the other, and long bridges. I was impressed with the view.

Because of my physical disability, I need to wear the correct shoes, but they were always hard to get. When we arrived at the bodega, the ground was covered with snow. While I was trying to walk from Papi's car to the bodega, my shoes came off and Papi had to carry me on his back. My feet froze, and I had to sit by an electrical heater in my uncle's bodega.

Ten People, One Roof: My First Home in America

When Mami, my brothers, and I arrived in Paterson, we lived in a crowded house. In order to save money on rent, electrical bills, and other expenses, my family decided to rent a big house so everybody would live under the same roof. My parents, brothers, grandparents, Soris, another aunt, an uncle, and I all moved in together.

It was crazy living with so many people. Money was also tight for my grandparents, because their three younger grown kids had moved to New Jersey a month earlier. With the support of Mami's brother, Marino, his former wife Damaris, and Mami's parents, the family immigrated to New Jersey.

The 10 of us lived in a single-family house for a few months. Upstairs were three bedrooms and a bathroom. The living room, kitchen, and a half bathroom were downstairs. The master bedroom, where my grandparents slept, was also downstairs. Sometimes to take a shower, we had to get in line.

During the day, I stayed home with my grandmother. Mami got a job in a factory near home within a week. My brothers started school. The rest of the relatives were gone for work. I had to wait before I could start school, since I would be enrolled under special education and had to go through a special process.

On my second day in the US, I was expecting to eat a heavy meal at lunchtime. My body was in Paterson, but my mind was in the DR. Instead of eating *arroz* and h*abichuela* at noon, I would have to wait until dinner. Lunch was a lighter meal in the US.

At 3:00 p.m., I smelled the aroma of seasoning, oregano, onion, pepper, and meat cooking. I saw Abuela Gregoria in the kitchen holding a large spoon and, at the side of the pot of meat, another pot boiling with beans. On the table was a bowl with rice ready to be cooked. I asked her, "*¿Porque estás cocinando ese tipo de comida tan tarde?*" (Why are you cooking that type of meal so late?)

Abuela replied, "*Casi todo el mundo se pasa el dia trabajando. Yo estoy cocinando temprano comparado con otras personas.* (Almost everybody spends the day working and after they come home, they cook.)

In fact, Abuela said she was making dinner early compared to some Americans who cook after they get home from work, at 5:30 p.m. or even later. At the time, Abuela's explanation didn't make sense to me, but I had to get used to it. This is the custom of my new country.

Adjusting to American Culture While Remembering My Native Culture.

The teen years are usually tough, but especially when the teenager is also learning the way of life in another country. At first, I felt confused and unsure about who I was and where I belonged. I was moving from childhood toward adulthood and from Dominican to Dominican-American. It was a time I rejected being an immigrant, a Dominican, or a Dominican-American; I only wanted to be myself. Despite all my doubts, I tried to be a typical 15-year-old girl.

In early fall 1988, my parents rented a small apartment in Paterson. They, my two brothers, and I moved out of the crowded house on 16th Street and into our own space.

CHAPTER 3

Father & Daughter Reunited

My early memories of Papi were comforting, the way the aroma of fresh bread just out of the oven can be. I recalled him living with the family in the DR. He used to work as a bus driver for one of those little buses that we called *asomiba*. At the end of the day, he came home with the newspaper he liked to read. Sometimes he also came home around noon for lunch. Afterwards, he sat in his rocking chair to have a little siesta, with his mouth open and a toothpick inside. Because he worked so much, I really didn't get to know him very well.

The man that I met again, years later in America, was my father who was giving me financial support. I was living in his house, but his absence, due to long hours at work, made the situation similar to what it was back in the DR. Papi worked as a gypsy cab driver in the Bronx, seven days a week. He commuted every day from Paterson. I didn't understand why Papi had to work the way he did. In the beginning, when I asked him why he didn't come home early, Papi's response was that there were bills to pay and food to buy.

After four years, of not being able to see him because we lived in different countries, I wasn't satisfied with his answer. I hoped that by asking these questions, I could change the situation and make him want to come home earlier, but my hands were tied. Things were not going to change.

I really wanted a hug from him and a long conversation. I wanted to become closer and somehow try to make up for the years we spent apart. Not seeing Papi from the age of 11 to 15 felt like a decade to me. The first few weeks after we arrived in the US, there were a couple of evenings when Papi came home early, at 8 o'clock. My brothers and I already had dinner. He sat down and ate, while Mami sat by him. My brothers and I waited eagerly for Papi to get home. Once he arrived, we followed him around the house like puppies, just so we could be with him for a while.

The relationship between Papi and me was not the type of father/daughter relationship I desired and tried to build when I asked him why he was working so many hours every day. I wanted to spend more time with Papi. At age 15, I was a señorita, but still the wanted to be daddy's girl. I was like an abandoned puppy that looks for love and protection. When we met again, I thought it would be that way, but I was wrong. I realized that was just a fantasy.

At that age, four years was a very long time to not see your father. It was hard getting to know his personality again, his favorite food, his hobbies, his way of talking, and everything else about him. I felt that I was not getting to know Papi, and this was hard.

I still didn't know much about him. Whatever I knew about Papi's personality was mostly from the short conversations we had over the phone a few times a month, when he called the family in the DR from New York and told me to be a good girl for Mami. Or when Mami talked to my brothers and to me about Papi.

Back in the DR, after Papi moved to New York, Papi's father, Jose Antonio "Don Toton," played the role of a father to us. Each time my younger brother had to be rushed to the doctor, because he got sick unexpectedly with high fever, Abuelo went along with Mami.

A month after I moved to Paterson, I had an experience that made me feel emotionally connected to Papi. I got a letter from Abuelo, replying to a letter that I wrote earlier to him. I was sitting at the kitchen table reading the letter and started to cry. I felt Papi's arms from behind me, reaching around my neck giving me a hug, while his eyes started watering, too.

I was feeling a mix of emotions. I felt sad, because I was missing Abuelo. I felt happy too, because I was connecting to Papi at that moment. He understood how I was feeling, since he was missing his father too.

In the letter Abuelo told me to study hard, so someday I could become a doctor and be able to take care of him when he got sick. Those words meant a lot to me and still do. I never actually considered becoming a doctor, and I don't think Abuelo meant that seriously. It was his way of motivating me to obtain a college degree. Abuelo always encouraged the younger generation to pursue higher education.

Based on the few conversations that I had with Papi about Abuelo, I realized how much Papi loved his father and how proud he felt. Papi remembered Abuelo's unique personality, especially when it came to his role as a father and as a partner. Abuelo always let Papi's mother know where he was going and what time he would be returning home, especially during the Trujillo dictatorship back in the 50s. At that time, anyone caught out on the street would be arrested and had to spend the rest of the night in jail, even if he wasn't doing anything wrong.

Abuelo was a tall, dark man with a big heart. He always cared for his family and his friends. He was the kind of person who was by your side whenever you needed him. He didn't earn any college degrees, but his words were full of wisdom obtained through years of life experience.

He also was very concerned about his appearance. He used to wear a nice short-sleeved shirt, regular long pants, or a long *guayabera (*formal shirt*)* with a pocket. He was always clean-shaven and never went out without a fedora on his head. Abuelo was one of the few people I ever saw in the DR who wore a formal black suit for special occasions, such as a wedding.

Three years later, I had another experience where I felt emotionally connected to Papi. Abuelo got sick and had to undergo surgery. I thought he would get well, but things did not go that way. I didn't know a lot about his illness, and this was a sensitive topic, rarely discussed at home. As time passed, Abuelo didn't recover the way he was supposed to.

Papi and I never talked with each other about the situation. I didn't know how to approach him to talk about Abuelo's illness. Papi and I had spent four years without seeing each other. During that period a phone line was the only connection that existed between us. Once we met again, there was still not a lot spoken between us.

Even though in Paterson Papi and I lived in the same house, we remained disconnected emotionally. Everything

I knew was based on the conversations Papi had with other relatives. This was the first time I had to deal with a major illness in my family.

All the news coming from the DR was bad. Abuelo didn't get out of bed. He stopped eating. He was growing weaker. On a Saturday morning in late June, Mami told me the truth after Papi had left for work early. The night before, after I went to bed, my parents got a phone call from Abuelo's family, saying that my grandfather was in agony.

I was in denial. Despite the advanced stage of his illness, I was hoping for a miracle to happen, like in the stories that I had heard about people being near death, but suddenly recovering. The same could happen to Abuelo, I hoped.

At 4:00 p.m. on Saturday, the phone rang and Mami answered. Papi's youngest brother, Arcenio, was calling from DR. The ring of the phone told me the sad news, before Mami did. The miracle did not happen. Abuelo had just passed away. I broke down in tears.

I thought of Papi, who hadn't been able to go visit Abuelo, and now would never be able to see his father again. Papi was working when the news came. Mami reached him by phone.

One more time, Papi and I felt connected and closer than ever. When he arrived home we hugged each other and cried. I grew up hearing people saying "*los hombers no lloran.*" Men don't cry. If they do cry, it is considered a weakness. Women are the ones who are allowed to express their feelings. Men should be tough and macho. Maybe this was the reason why Papi and I were so distant from each other. But at this time of pain, we came together.

I did not learn the cause of Abuelo's death until years later, when relatives told me he died from cancer. I was about to turn 19, and this was the first time I lost a loved one who was so close to me. Being far away and unable to go through the mourning rituals and attend the services for Abuelo made the grieving period even harder. Only time healed the emotional wound that ached in me for a very long while.

CHAPTER 4

EDUCATION AND EXPECTATIONS

Before I moved to Paterson, I knew I would have the opportunity to go to school, but I couldn't start immediately. I was already in a country where I could become educated, yet I had to keep waiting. It was easy to say, but hard to do.

During the first few weeks, I became depressed. I stayed home all day with Abuela. There was not much to do at home in Paterson in the middle of winter. Looking out the window, all I saw were dead trees and closed doors. I hated being stuck inside the house.

I slept 10 hours straight every day. Mami worked at a nearby factory and when she came home for lunch, I was still in bed. "*¿Juana que te pasa? Levantate son las 12:00 del dia.*" Juana what is wrong with you?" she asked. "It is 12 o'clock already." I yawned, "OK, Mami ya me voy a levantar." OK, Mami I will get up.

My dream of getting an education hadn't come true yet, and I didn't have much to do. I helped Abuela around the house or watched "novela," soap operas in Spanish. From the beginning, Mami was involved in a long process of finding the right school for me. Papi was too busy working as a cab driver to help her with that.

We were living in the US for only a month and didn't know what steps to take to get me enrolled in school. Mami was working in the daytime and wasn't driving yet, so we often had to ask somebody to drive us if there was a certain place we needed to go.

One day Mami and I had to go to the Paterson Board of Health to get information regarding the immunization shots required to attend school. A family friend drove Mami and me to the Board of Health. After we arrived, Mami and our friend went to find information. In the meantime. I sat down to wait in an area where other people were also waiting. We were supposed to take a ticket with a number then wait until our number was called.

While I was sitting, everybody got up to get their tickets including those who arrived last. When Mami came back, she asked me for her ticket, but my hands were empty. I was afraid of getting out of the chair to walk the few steps to take a ticket. It was the first time that I had to do something on my own in public, and I wasn't ready yet. Mami went to get the ticket instead.

Evaluations

I realized that certain things would be difficult for me to accomplish, even the most common ones, like attending school. It was easy to understand, but hard to accept. Now that I was in the US and could go to school, we had to find the right school for me. It was a process that took nine months.

The first place Mami tried was School 21 in Paterson, the school that my brothers attended, and she got some information to get the process started. Then Mami, Damaris (Mami's former sister-in-law), and I visited the school.

We were introduced to the child study team that included a social worker, a psychologist and a learning specialist. The experts said evaluations were the appropriate way to find out what school I should attend, so I went through different types of evaluations: psychological, physical, and opthamological, among others, all conducted by the team. These procedures were all new to me. I didn't understand what was going on. All I knew was that I would finally be able to attend school.

According to the team, I would be enrolled in special education. A few days before I started my education, I had the opportunity to visit the school that I would attend. I had one more evaluation there. This one was conducted by an Italian woman. Even though I spoke only Spanish, I was able to communicate with her, since Italian is similar.

We met in a small room near the school entrance. I didn't have a chance to walk through most of the school, but my expectations were really high. After nine months, all the paperwork was done and I was ready to start my education. I was very excited.

CHAPTER 5

CP CENTER

In November 1988, a couple of months after I had turned 16, a yellow bus arrived at my home to pick me up and take me to the Elks Cerebral Palsy Center in the nearby city of Clifton. The bus arrived at the school a few minutes after 9:00 a.m. All the other students were already in their classrooms.

My mental image of a classroom came from my brothers' school photos and from TV shows. Alfredo and Benito were in different grades, and their school photos showed each wearing his uniform while sitting at a desk. Nothing in their photos or the TV programs prepared me for what I saw: A whole a group of students with disabilities in a classroom all together. Half of the room was set up as a classroom with a blackboard, a couple of regular desks, and a few adaptive desks for those students in wheelchairs. The other half was still a regular living room.

There were nine students in the class, and only one other who was Hispanic. Mily was from Puerto Rico, but most of the time she spoke English. It was a little easier for me to communicate with the teacher, Miss Maria, who was from Italy. At the CP Center I learned independent living skills as well as academic subjects. We learned how to prepare a sandwich, count money, do housekeeping tasks, and write checks. Therapy sessions were also part of my education. Once a week, I had physical therapy, speech therapy, and occupational therapy.

Even though the classmates treated me nicely, I had to deal with the language barrier and cultural differences. I wanted to be like many of my classmates who were familiar with the culture and communicated easily with one another. During the first year, I felt like an outsider, whose only desire was to fit in. No matter how hard I tried to understand my teacher and my classmates, I could not and felt terrible. I started to hate being in school. Every day I looked forward to the time when the school bus would come and take me back home.

The next September I came back after summer vacation and found out that Miss Maria was no longer my teacher. I was concerned about how I would communicate with the new teacher, Miss Angela. The CP Center was a small school and didn't offer ESL courses (English As a Second Language). Students were assigned to their classrooms based on their ages which ranged from 16 to 21. Each class had both a teacher and an aide. Most of the day, my classmates and I remained in the classroom, working on school projects.

Sometimes we worked in groups with students from other classes. For one project, we learned about different methods for protecting the environment, such as recycling newspapers. We also collaborated on artistic projects and performed plays. All the classes would gather together at lunchtime, and for special holiday celebrations, like Thanksgiving, Christmas, Halloween, and Valentine's Day.

Subjects such as English, math, social science, and natural science were covered occasionally. Even though I was in the classroom with the older students, the lessons were taught at a low level due to the learning disabilities of some of my classmates. I paid close attention to Miss Angela each time she taught a lesson related to social or natural science. However, the language was still a barrier, since I still only had learned basic vocabulary in English.

I knew that somehow I had to understand the language better to learn the school material. Plus, I needed to communicate with my classmates, Miss Angela, the teacher's assistant, and my therapists. I came up with an idea. It didn't solve my problem completely, but it did help me a little.

At home, twice at week, I grabbed an English and Spanish dictionary and looked up words that might be useful for me to know. I wrote down words like moon, stars, people and community. Many of these words had come up during class lessons. The next day I would show my list to Miss Angela. Together, we reviewed the words. I practiced pronouncing them and also learned their definitions.

I also gained some work experience at the CP Center. I volunteered to make coffee in the kitchen and also helped the receptionist once a week with filing and other office duties. One very special responsibility was to help assist one student who was in a wheelchair and unable to talk. I enjoyed getting this experience and knowing that I was helping others.

Becoming Part of the Community

Mami had left her factory job and now worked part-time cleaning offices in the evening, so she was able to be home at the time I returned from school. I was not a little kid anymore, but it was a family rule that somebody had to be home by the time the school bus dropped me off. Mami, Papi, my brothers, and I were now living in a three-bedroom apartment that my parents rented in Paterson.

One spring morning, Mami had a meeting with my brother Alfredo's teacher. He was enrolled in ESL was struggling to learn the new language, so this teacher referred Mami to an organization that helped Hispanic parents who had children in school.

Mami called and talked with the secretary, who invited her to attend weekly meetings. Mami asked me to go with her. The meetings were held on Saturdays from 2:00 to 4:00 p.m. at what was then a branch of the public library in Paterson.

The first meeting we attended was in May 1990, a day before Mother's Day. When Mami and I arrived, people were sitting in a big circle. The woman in charge introduced herself as Doña Ligia, founder of "La Asociación Del Hispano Inpedido de New Jersey" (The Hispanic Association with for People with Disabilities of New Jersey). She invited us to sit down and join the group.

After the introduction, Doña Ligia said that in the 70s, she came from Ecuador with her son, Juan Carlos, who had Down syndrome. Due to the struggles that Doña Ligia and Juan Carlos went through, she was inspired to help other families going through similar situations. It was around the late 70s when she founded La Asociación Del Hispano Inpedido de New Jersey. At that time, she was working for The Multilingual Center, run by Catholic Family & Community Services (CFCS), which supported Ligia's organization, even though it was an independent project.

The following day, La Asociacion celebrated Mother's Day with a special performance by young adults. They danced the Lambada, the hottest pop song and dance at the moment. I was very impressed to see people with disabilities performing that way. Mami and I decided to join the organization. Every week La Asociacion held a different type of event. I had the option to go off with the young people and children or stay in the workshops with Mami. I chose to stay. It was at these meetings that I met David and his mother, who were also members. Years later, David and I became close friends.

Some of the workshops focused on education and were led by experts in the field. One of the topics discussed was Individualized Education Plan (IEP). Neither Mami nor I knew the meaning of that term, but we would learn more about that in my future educational journey.

At the same time, at the CP Center I was exceeding all expectations despite not having attended school in the past. During the five years I attended the Center, I learned the basics of using the computer and gained work experience by helping the receptionist. In addition, I wrote about my culture whenever we had a cultural event. Once a week we were asked to read the newspaper and bring an article to class the next day and discuss it.

In late winter 1993, Mami asked Rosita Kardashian, then the new director of the Multilingual Center, if one of the persons in charge of advocacy could attend the annual IEP meeting at the school. At the meeting were Mami, a former advocate named Daisy, a teacher, the school principal, the social worker, and me.

Daisy suggested that I be transferred to a regular high school, because I had the potential to succeed there. One of the requirements of IEP was to establish new goals for the students. Transferring to a new school became my goal. The suggestion emerged in part because of the Americans With Disabilities Act (ADA) passed in 1990, two years after I started school. For people with disabilities, the ADA was similar to the 1964 Civil Rights Act for racial justice.

Mami signed the authorization to get started with the process. Even though I was 20, Mami was still my legal guardian. The idea of attending a regular high school sounded scary, but at the same time exciting. So I agreed. I knew it would be a challenge, but something inside said, "Try"

The following day, Daisy initiated the paperwork. This meant that I would be attending a new school in September. I had the option to choose from the three high schools in the area. Eastside High School and John F. Kennedy High School were both located in the city of Paterson. My other option was Passaic County Technical Institute in Wayne, a suburban community nearby. Mami and I visited each high school, accompanied by Daisy or Rosita.

For Mami and me, there were so many unanswered questions. How could I walk among the crowd of students from one classroom to the next one? What would happen if I fell down? I take longer doing my class work. What if the teacher gave me an assignment to do in class and I could not complete it on time?

Even worse, I heard horrible stories describing high school as an environment full of fights, where students cut classes all the time, had sex, and used illegal drugs. Some people reacted negatively to my plan to attend regular high school, but despite their criticism, I decided to move forward, I wanted to keep the commitment that I had made to myself and to others, like Abuelo, that I would get an education.

The day to choose which school I would attend was fast approaching. I would have to decide on my own among the three choices. I knew that regardless of the school I chose, I would be the oldest student there. The day of the big decision arrived; I had carefully analyzed the pros and cons of each school and decided to attend John F. Kennedy High School. In JFK, all the classes would be in one building. I would not have to walk from one building to another and the school environment didn't seem as bad as in the stories I had heard. I was finally ready.

CHAPTER 6

A Regular High School Student

In November 1993, the Monday after Thanksgiving, I experienced a major change as a student. I was no longer attending the CP Center, which was not actually a high school. For the first time, I was enrolled in a traditional school environment. Attending high school was a big challenge and, at the same time, a rewarding experience.

The new school was huge, especially compared to the CP Center. In the Center, all the classrooms and offices were on one floor. JFK had three floors. After the bus dropped me off, I walked straight to the child study team office to meet with my social worker, Ms. Weitzman, before class.

We rode the elevator to the third floor where Ms. Weitzman walked me to my homeroom and introduced me to my homeroom teacher. I learned that every morning, high school students had to report to homeroom for attendance. Then, Ms. Weitzman and I walked to Room 316 where we met Ms. Valentin, who would assist me in my classes. Ms. Valentin was with me all day. She took notes for me and also helped me with math, my most difficult subject.

Most of the classes I took were in the special education category and had about ten students and a teacher's aide per class. I was the only special ed student with physical limitations and a personal aide. Some of my classmates had learning disabilities or behavioral issues.

In contrast with my schooling at the CP Center, at JFK, I was able to take English, math, history, health, science, and music, among other classes. I was eager to learn and spent plenty of time doing my class lessons and my homework. When I wasn't able to complete class assignments on time, I asked my teachers to let me take the work home and bring it to them the next day. Since freshman year, I earned mostly As and Bs on my report cards.

Then, another obstacle came up. Since I was 20 years old and the age limit for a student to receive special education was 21, I could stay in high school for only one year. With the support of Rosita Kardashian and Daisy Mendoza, then the director and the advocate from the Multilingual Center, Mami and I requested permission from the Paterson Board of Education for me to complete all four years of high school at JFK. Months later, the request was approved and my age was no longer an obstacle to getting my high school education.

To my classmates, I didn't look older. None of them knew my real age. When any of them asked how old I was, I told them that I was 17 or 18. Also, aside from Ms. Valentin, only a couple of the teachers knew my real age.

I was the only student with a personal assistant by my side all the time, but I don't think my classmates realized Ms. Valentin was an assistant. In fact, when she took a day off, they would ask me where my mom was. My initial fears about not being able to make it were vanishing as time moved on. Every morning after homeroom, Ms. Valentin and I walked from one classroom to the next. To avoid walking among the crowd of students who were changing classes, we usually left class a couple of minutes early.

But this was not always possible. Sometimes, we had to stay to the end of the class, especially when I was taking a test. Most of the classes took place on the third floor, while others were on the first floor, so we had to take the elevator. Ms. Valentin was authorized to carry an elevator key and I was the only student allowed to ride.

When the elevator wasn't working, and we had to use the stairs instead or when there was a fire drill, Ms. Valentin and I were always the last ones to make it to the first floor. Fortunately, nothing serious ever happened.

Health Class

Health was one of my favorite subjects. I enjoyed learning about the human body, particularly the reproductive system and the process of puberty. It was liberating to learn about these topics, because at home, my family rarely mentioned the word sex. In my culture, sexuality was not discussed openly.

In class I always sat in the first row, with my book open. On a typical school day, Carlos Lugo, the teacher, began the class by explaining why safe sex was important. Then he listed the consequences of unsafe sex such as getting pregnant, or becoming infected with a sexually transmitted disease like chlamydia, gonorrhea, genital herpes, and HIV/AIDS. Mr. Lugo stressed the importance of safe sex for both girls and boys.

Mr. Lugo's personality was one of his great qualities. His enthusiasm for his students was contagious. It was impossible to feel bored in his class. Mr. Lugo taught us about more than just how the body works. He also taught us how to have healthy attitudes. He explained how important it is to have high self-esteem and suggested that his students look in the mirror every morning and say, "I am important. I am unique. I'm worthy as a person." This was a way to create a positive image about ourselves.

Mr. Lugo encouraged the class to look with optimism toward the future and to set goals despite any challenges or criticism we might face. I felt especially motivated when he encouraged everyone in class to attend college. I never before heard any of my teachers mention a word about attending college. His advice made a strong impression on me.

In addition to my academic studies, I also had physical therapy once or twice a week at the high school. Jim was my physical therapist and our sessions were held on the first floor in the main hallway where people could see me as I followed Jim's instructions on how to walk. One day while I was having therapy, my school counselor passed by and saw me walking back and forth, trying to step with my heel down, following Jim's instructions.

The counselor approached us and asked me if I preferred to go to another spot where I would not be seen. When I replied that I would, I had no idea what that would lead to. She looked for a hidden place by the auditorium, where I could hardly be seen by others. Jim and I followed her to the spot. A couple of minutes later, when the counselor left, Jim set up two chairs, one for himself and one for me.

I saw the expression on his face and realized that he was not happy. Jim looked me straight in the eye and asked me if I was satisfied with my counselor's suggestion. I replied yes. I didn't know much English yet, but Jim's body language said it all. He was very upset. Then, he told me, "Tomorrow don't come to school. Stay home."

At that moment I realized that I shouldn't have accepted my counselor's suggestion. The next day, Jim came back and apologized. We continued our sessions in the hallway. From that moment on, the counselor didn't mention anything, even if she saw Jim and me in the hallway.

As a young adult, I had just learned one of the most important lessons in my life. I learned that although I had cerebral palsy, I shouldn't hide myself from others. I have to accept myself in order for others to accept Juana. Now, I realize the irony of the situation, because in spite of having been accepted by my family, at that moment I didn't accept myself and I wanted to hide.

Jim passed away a few years later. I wish I could go back in time and thank him for what he taught me. Back then I was immature and took for granted the valuable lessons he tried to teach me. Jim wasn't just a therapist. He was also a friend, who always accepted me for who I was.

My Story Reaches the Media

During my sophomore year at JFK, a story about me and a photo appeared in two local major newspapers, *The Record* and *The Herald-News*, both published by the same media outlet, North Jersey Media Group. The article ran in their "Student of the Week" feature.

I was surprised to find out that someone from the school office had contacted the newspaper about me. I wasn't a famous singer or a movie star, so why would they want to interview me? I learned that they were interested, because I wasn't a typical high school student. So, on a cold February morning in 1995, the news reporter and I met at the high school library.

Ms. Valentin sat beside me during the interview. The reporter asked her a few questions related to my classes, but most of his questions were for me. My English skills were still weak, and my speech was not clear due to the CP, so I expected to feel nervous, but I wasn't. For some strange reason, I felt confident and relaxed during the interview.

After all these years, I sometimes look back and re-read the article, which told about my experience as an immigrant with a disability who wanted to get an education. The article also included my comment that at one time, I couldn't imagine myself attending high school, but here I was. Reading this statement made me realize how far I had come.

It is good to recall these moments from the past. Sometimes I get so focused on what I am going doing right now that I forget how significant my previous accomplishments were. Reading the article reminded me that it was a major achievement, at the time of that interview, for me to be attending high school, speaking English, and having an interview with a newspaper reporter.

When the article was published, it was read by many people around New Jersey. I realized how they came to know about some of my life experiences through the written word.

Some people said they saw me as a role model, although I didn't see it that way at the time.

A few days after the article appeared in the paper, Mr. Lugo, my health teacher, told me that I would be getting an award from a local organization for my achievement. I didn't understand why. I didn't see anything extraordinary about my life. All I was trying to do was obtain my high school diploma like everybody else. Except I was in my early 20s and had CP.

A month later, I received The Dominican Excellence Award from the *Asociación pro Desarrollo de los Dominicanos* (Dominicans Development Association), due to my outstanding efforts to succeed in school. The award was presented on a Sunday evening in a formal ceremony at the Paterson Museum. Mami and Papi attended.

At the ceremony, there were others who also received recognition for their contributions to the community, but I was the only student to be honored. Mr. Lugo, a founder of the organization was also the master of ceremonies. I was called to come up front where I received a small trophy. When Mr. Lugo read a brief biography about me to the audience, I received a standing ovation. My eyes filled with tears. I had never experienced anything like this before.

A few years later, I interviewed Mr. Lugo for one of my journalism classes. My assignment for the class was to interview some people who knew me, but to ask the questions as though I were writing about someone else. When I asked Mr. Lugo why Juana Ortiz received that award in 1995, he replied, "Juana received an award from a Dominican organization in recognition of her excellence, and for her outstanding efforts to succeed in life."

Ms. Valentin and Senior Year

The academic year 1996-97 was an exciting one for me. I was a high school senior and graduation was right around the corner. I never imagined that I would one day experience this moment. By then, Ms. Valentin and I had a special bond. To me, she was not just a teacher's aide or special ed assistant; she was also a teacher and a mentor who walked with me on this high school journey that was coming to a happy end.

My classmates often thought she was my mother, and she could have been, since her older daughter was my age. Because Ms. Valentin was Puerto Rican and I was Dominican, our cultural connection as well as compatible personalities enabled us to get along easily.

She motivated me to study hard and pursue a college degree. These words of hers have remained with me to this day: *"Tu pareja te puede dejar, los hijos uno los tiene pero no son de uno. Pero lo que tu aprendas es tuyo y nadie te lo puede quitar."* (Your partner can walk away. We might have kids, but we don't own them. All that you learn will always be yours, and nobody can take it away from you).

Those days in math class when a simple division problem seemed impossible for me to understand, Ms Valentin sat next to me, grabbed a piece of scrap paper and, with a lot of patience, explained several times how to divide 4 into 12 or how to multiply 6 oranges by 3. I did a few examples as homework, too. But the next day in class, when I was asked by the math teacher to try the same problem with higher numbers, I had trouble following the correct steps. Math was always a challenge for me, even with Ms. Valentin's help.

English class was the opposite. I didn't need to do the same assignment over and over, as I did in math. After the teacher gave the instructions and Ms. Valentin explained them to me in Spanish, I completed the assignments easily. In my English class, the major focus was on learning various words and their definitions. Many of the terms were new to me. When we covered the parts of speech, I would write sentences with nouns, verbs, adjectives, and so on.

Then, I would re-write a paragraph. The materials were in English, and my academic skills were improving. One drawback was the lack of resources. JFK was a public school in a poor district; we didn't have our own textbooks. There were only a few books available, and I had to share them with my classmates.

I decided to create my own resources. At home I read newspapers to help improve my language skills. I decided to subscribe for one year to a local newspaper. Every night after dinner I read the paper with an English-Spanish dictionary alongside me. I underlined words that I did not understand and looked up the translation.

My High School Sweetheart

We were freshmen when we first met one autumn morning at the school bus on our way to high school back in 1993. Persio always sat at the back of the bus by the window, and I sat in front. I rarely heard him talking with other students aboard the bus. I was five years older than Persio, since I started high school at age 20. He was in two of my special ed classes and he never missed a day. He always wore a nice shirt, jeans, and white sneakers.

Outside class, Persio hung out with a Hispanic guy, Rene, but at school he kept to himself and was quiet. During sophomore year, Persio and I had lunch at the same time, but he sat at a different table, by himself. He was shy, so one day Ms Valentin stepped in and invited him to sit at my lunch table. Since they knew each other, it was easier for Persio to talk to Ms. Valentin. From then on, he and I had lunch together at the same table.

We loved talking to each other and discovered we were both from the DR, but different cities. He came from Santiago. Since the bus dropped us off early at school, Ms Valentin and I went straight upstairs to the special ed department and waited in a classroom until it was time to go to homeroom at 8.15 a.m. The rest of the students hung out outside of the building. Only students with permission from the teachers or security were allowed to go upstairs before class started. While we were waiting, Persio would join us. He grabbed a chair, sat next to me, and we chatted. By the end of junior year, we had become very good friends.

Persio and his mother had arrived in Paterson, when he was nine months old He was diagnosed with glaucoma and needed specialized medical care that was not available in the DR. Due to the medical care Persio received in the US, his vision improved significantly, but he was still visually impaired. I invited him to join the parents' advocacy group that Mami and I had joined.

Meantime, Persio and I saw each other every day at school and continued our conversations about our classes, teachers, and current events. It was already senior year and the prom was coming up. Most of our classmates were planning to attend, some with a date others with a group of friends. Persio and I were not very active socially within the school. For people with disabilities, it was hard to fit in socially at a regular high school, especially when there is also a language barrier.

My Senior Prom

Sometimes it was hard for me to have a sense of where I really belonged. Even though I was several years older than my classmates, I didn't look like a 24-year-old. I didn't feel like one either. Regardless of my age, I was a high school student and, like the others, I wanted to experience the prom, just like our classmates who would be there with their friends or dates.

Since we didn't have many school friends, Persio and I would be going by ourselves to the prom, so I thought we probably should go together, but I didn't think it would be appropriate to ask a guy to be my prom date. One afternoon while he and I were waiting for the school bus, Ms. Valentin intervened again and suggested that we go together to the prom. Thanks to her, we agreed it was a good idea and decided to be prom dates.

For most girls, finding the right prom gown was a major job. For me, it was not a problem. I went shopping with Mami and saw a dark blue gown I liked right away. I tried it on and, and it fit me perfectly. In my case, finding the right shoes for the prom was a bigger concern. Due to the CP, I can't wear high heels, though I would like to. Finding comfortable but pretty dress shoes was always a problem. Mami and I shopped at a few stores for the right pair.

I had another concern. What if we find the right shoes, but the color doesn't match? I didn't have much experience with buying formal clothing, but Ms. Valentin told me that shoes can be dyed to match the dress color. Then Mami worried that the people in charge of coloring the shoe might accidentally dye it the wrong shade. That got me worried. I could end up wearing shoes that were a different color from the gown. What was I going to do? After all that worrying, we went to a store where we found shoes that matched the gown and fit me perfectly. I even found a matching purse. I was ready for my senior prom.

Prom Night

Neither Persio nor I could drive, so Papi took us to the prom. First we stopped at Persio's house to pick him up. I was used to seeing Persio wearing jeans, shirts, and sneakers. Seeing him wearing a tuxedo that matched the color of my gown was like seeing a different person. I thought he looked handsome, but I didn't feel confident enough to say so, especially since he was shy. I didn't want to embarrass him. We did not make any comment to each another about our prom night appearance, but Persio bought me a pretty wrist corsage with a small flower. For me that was very special.

The evening was full of excitement for the two of us. Papi dropped us at the front entrance of The West Paterson County Club, now known as the Westmount Country Club, in Woodland Park, a town near Paterson. When Persio and I walked inside, Ms. Valentin was in the main lobby and directed us toward the professional photographer who would take our prom photo. Even though she was waiting for me, Ms. Valentin didn't play the role of a chaperone. After the photo session ended, she told me, "This is your evening," meaning I was not in class. I was there to have fun, like the rest of the seniors.

Then, dinner was served. The elegant tables, the shiny dance floor, sparkling lights, festive decorations, and happy people around us made me feel like a teenager who, for the first time, goes out with her friends. Persio and I danced to "Latinos," one of the hottest songs of the 90s by Projecto Uno, a famous Dominican-American group. Their music style was a mix of different genres, and it made me want to dance.

Throughout the evening, Persio and I socialized with our classmates and teachers. Neither of us had much opportunity to socialize before, and we were having fun doing it now. We danced, took photos, laughed, and talked. It was our big night, and I enjoyed being by Persio's side dancing until it was time to leave.

When the prom was over, Papi dropped Persio off, then we went home. I washed my face, put my pajamas on and went to bed. I hugged my pillow, feeling pleased for the wonderful time that I had and fell asleep happy.

High School Graduation: I Made It!

Being close to obtaining my high school diploma was an amazing feeling. Even more amazing was that as the school year drew to an end, I was honored with several awards for my academic achievement. I received one from a group of disability activists and another from the former mayor of the city of Paterson, Bill Pascrell, who is currently a Congressman.

Graduation day arrived. June 20, 1997. I could hardly believe this day had finally come. To mark the occasion, Mami decorated my room with balloons and flowers. On the night table were cards, a teddy bear, and a photo album that Ms. Valentin crafted especially for me as a graduation gift. It had a white cover which she decorated with tiny caps in black and red, the school colors.

Ms. Valentin supported me all the way to this day, and she also admired my parents for raising me to be independent. As a special education aide and teacher, she had worked with students with disabilities whose families tend to overprotect them. She said to me, *"Yo felicito a tus padres por la manera en que te criaron. Porque no te sobre protegieron como suelen hacer algunos padres que tienen hijos con discapacidad."* (I give your parents credit for the way that they raised you. They didn't overprotect you as many parents tend to do when their kids have disabilities).

That hot summer evening, at Paterson's Hinchliffe Stadium, I marched in the John F. Kennedy High School Class of 1997 and received my high school diploma at age 24. My dream came true. My parents, my aunt Soris, and my brother Alfredo were there to cheer my achievement. After the ceremony, Mami took photos, while I held my diploma and smiled. Each photo showed my pride. Over and over, I kept repeating, "I made it! I made it!"

To celebrate, my family and I went to the Bronx for dinner at El Rey Del Marisco, a restaurant that specialized in seafood and used to be one of my favorite dining places. Though the restaurant has since closed, it will always be special to me, because I celebrated my high school graduation there.

With my high school goal achieved, I started thinking of my next step. During my senior year, I had seen many of my classmates visiting the offices of the high school counselors. They held in their hands applications for colleges, scholarships, and jobs. Although Ms. Valentin and Dr. Lugo had encouraged me to register for college, I worried that at college I would not have anyone to help me the way that Ms. Valentin did. I would not be enrolled in special education, either. Despite these doubts, the idea of registering for college grew in my mind. Earning a college degree sounded so exciting. There was that internal voice telling me: "Try, try."

I always had a close relationship with my mother and usually turned to her first when I needed good advice. Although I had support from both of my parents, I first asked Mami what she thought about my attending college. Then I asked Papi. Both agreed to support my new goal.

In April 1997, during spring break, I asked Mami to go with me to Passaic County Community College (PCCC) in downtown Paterson. That was the first of many trips Mami and I would make to the college. With the assistance of a PCCC staff member, I filled out the application. A few days later, I received a letter notifying me of the date for my required placement test.

My optimism started to grow, but I still had some concerns. Would other prospective students be taking the test, too? What if I ran out of time? I kept asking all these questions as Mami drove me to Passaic County Community College (PCCC) for my test.

CHAPTER 7

STARTING COLLEGE

Once I was at PCCC, I took the elevator by myself to the second floor and walked to the writing lab. There were several computers, a couple of empty tables and a woman who identified herself in Spanish as Ivelisse, a tutor. It was mid-May and the spring semester had just ended, so there were no students around.

The placement test consisted of three parts: reading, writing, and math. While taking the test, I was very surprised to realize that it was not that hard. I was given extra time to complete the test. Then I submitted it and went home, hoping I did well enough to be accepted.

A couple of days later, I received an envelope from PCCC. I didn't open it right away. I was a little nervous that I might not be accepted. But I was anxious about being accepted, too. Could I handle the academic responsibilities of college on my own? I already knew that college life was very demanding, and in order to make it, I would have to work harder. I had some fears. Would I be able to understand the course material? How will the professors react to me? Will my classmates accept me?

I opened the envelope and happiness overcame anxiety. I had been accepted. Now I could start making plans to enter college in the fall. I still had concerns, but being accepted gave me courage. I was willing to take the risk, because I already made it through high school. If I was able to graduate from high school, why not to try to get a college degree, too?

After all I was in America and part of my American dream was to become well educated and financially independent. I wasn't sure if I would reach that goal, but at least I wanted to try. Maybe in the end I would succeed.

The next day I received a second letter from PCCC. This one was from the admissions counselor of the Educational Opportunity Fund (EOF) which offers certain students support in several areas like tutoring, advisement, and career planning. EOF also offers financial assistance to students who qualify and attend school full-time. I met with the counselor and learned more about joining EOF.

One of the requirements was to participate in a summer program designed to help students gain a better understanding of what college was like. The first event required participants to spend three days at nearby Montclair State University (MSU). This was the first time I would be far from home, surrounded by unfamiliar faces. I felt a little nervous, but I told myself if I want to go to college in America, I have to do it.

Mami supported my decision to attend the summer program, but she was not comfortable with the idea. On the way to PCCC where I would meet the other EOF students and board a bus to MSU, Mami told me, "If you hear or see anything unusual, please call home regardless of the time. We will come to pick you up."

We arrived at PCCC around 2:00 p.m. Two big yellow buses were parked by the entrance and a crowd of people was near the buses, some carrying small backpacks. I got aboard and took a seat. An hour later, the bus arrived at MSU where a couple of EOF counselors were waiting for us in the lobby. We were directed to a large table where the staff was waiting for the group to sign in. They gave me the key to my room, so I found my way there, unpacked my bag, and met my two roommates, Yozeti and Ibellise. Both girls were Hispanic and had recently finished high school, too. We liked each other right away.

Then, I went outside to meet with the group. We introduced ourselves. Many of the students were Hispanic and African-American and had graduated from local high schools or had completed the GED (high school equivalency) diplomas. I was the only person in the group who had a physical disability, but this time that didn't seem to matter. I felt welcomed by the others.

After the introductions, we had dinner. It was a nice, warm Sunday evening. The campus was huge and beautiful, and it was exciting to be on a college campus as a prospective student. I didn't know what lay ahead for me, but I felt happy. In two more days, I would start attending college at PCCC.

There was no need to call home. I stayed for the full three days at MSU, as planned. During those days, we played educational games, became better acquainted with each other, and learned a little about what college was like. We also registered for summer classes. In all, it was a great experience.

The next day, after we returned from MSU, I started taking classes at PCCC. The classes ran Mondays to Thursdays from 9:00 a.m. to 3:00 p.m. for five weeks. The students were divided into groups. I was among those whose main language was Spanish. The homework load seemed reasonable, and offered us a way to get warmed up for September. If I did well, I would not have to re-take the courses in the fall.

On Fridays, we went on field trips. Our visit to New York City included a Broadway show, the Barrio Museum, and a restaurant for lunch. The summer program was a good experience and gave me an idea about what to expect for the fall.

Fall Semester

It was a sunny September morning in 1997 that my next big dream would start to come true: I would be sitting in a college classroom as an enrolled student. Even after I moved to America, I didn't visualize myself attending college, because I was considered incapable of even fitting into a mainstream class. Due to the bureaucracy of the educational system, I felt that being enrolled automatically as a special education high school student prevented me from developing my full potential. It took me time and a lot of courage to break down those barriers.

Now I was a student at Passaic County Community College. I was excited, proud, and a little anxious. I struggled to get here, but didn't know what to expect and was unsure if I made the right decision by coming to college. I would soon find out.

My first class, and my only one of the day, started at 10:30 a.m. What we did as a class was introduce ourselves and review the course syllabus, which contained information about the course requirements and textbook. I was pleased that the professor, Ronnie Kaufman, was the same professor I had during the summer program. Some of my classmates from summer were in the class too, so that made the adjustment easier. After class was over Mami picked me up.

The next day, I really started to deal a little more with the college routine, especially the hurry of students and professors in the hallways, walking from one classroom to the next. For me, the walk took longer. This was my first time as a full-time student. Two of my classes met on the same day, but at least there was some time in between, so I could get from one class to the next in time.

I was taking classes in basic math, writing, reading, and grammar. All the courses were in the ESL category except for math. In addition, I attended a weekly lab for each of the classes. When a class ended, I walked straight to one of the labs and spent two to three hours there. I was expected to go for an hour, but I needed more time to complete the assignments.

Not all the challenges of college were academic. Even though I had taken a word processing computer class in high school, once I was in college I realized how weak my computer skills were. I did not even know how to save a file to a disk drive. When I was in the lab, I had to ask the tutor to save the file for me. As she was saving it, I watched her and tried to learn how to do it. One day I was in the writing lab and tried by myself to save the essay I was working on, but instead I deleted the material. I had to start all over again.

Another time, I tried to save the first draft of my assignment for my next lab session. It was part of the lab rule to write the final draft the following week. When I returned to finish the essay, I couldn't find the file because instead of saving it in the diskette, I saved it in the computer which another student was using when I arrived. Once again, I had to start all over, which caused me to stay in the lab longer as I tried to recall what I had written before.

In college, I discovered some weaknesses in my writing skills as well. My grammar was not very good, and I sometimes had a hard time writing a good thesis statement. Despite that, the tutors were impressed with my ideas, probably because my thoughts were logical and based on real experiences. I sat at my computer and just wrote what I thought was right.

When I started the third level (intermediate) of ESL, an English/Spanish dictionary became my best friend. I couldn't use the dictionary when taking a test, but I was allowed to ask the professors for correct spelling of words. Since I was still learning how to write in English, I made many errors in spelling, tenses, and other grammatical skills. My professors said I also did not provide enough details in my essays. I knew I needed to work more on skills.

On the other hand, I never had trouble with coming up with ideas to write about. When we were assigned a new topic, I quickly knew what I would write about, and I used my imagination to develop the ideas. If I were writing about my childhood, I tried to go back in time and recreate the scenes from my life, first in memories, then in words. I pictured myself in the past, as if I were living that moment again.

Writing that way came naturally to me and didn't seem like anything special, but that was not the reaction of my tutors and some of the ESL professors. They were noticing something special in my writing style that I wasn't aware of. But I still struggled with technical details.

As I was advancing to a higher academic level, the writing demands were becoming tougher. In fact, on a couple of occasions, certain professors believed that I should repeat a course, because they felt I was not ready for the next level.

I especially disliked writing outlines. In the lab and in class, I was expected to create an outline for every new essay. Unfortunately, that was one of my weaknesses. I took about 40 minutes to do an outline, yet I saw my classmates creating their outlines and showing them to the tutors and professors within a few minutes. I thought of an outline as similar to the blueprint of a design that the designer plans to show the potential buyer. The basic steps were to brainstorm, organize, order, and label. By the time I did all that and finished typing the first draft of the essay, I was tired!

I was then supposed to go back and re-read the essay, since it was easier to catch major errors at that point, but by then, I was often too tired to do the next step. I just handed in what I already had. Over time, I learned a new technique to deal with this. A couple of the ESL professors suggested keeping a journal and writing for at least ten minutes a few times weekly, without any interruption.

Every other day at home, I sat in front of my computer and I started typing about what I had done through the day.

I wrote even if there wasn't anything out of the ordinary to write about. Soon I realized that the technique was helping me organize my thoughts better. When I had to do an essay for class, I could skip the process of writing an outline whenever possible, but sometimes I just had to do it, because some professors required it. I also learned that I shouldn't immediately delete my first drafts, since some of the ideas there were better than in the revisions.

Becoming a better writer was a difficult process, but I appreciated the opportunity to improve. Even though I had recently graduated from high school, this was the first time that I was getting a good education regarding language skills. Back in my high school English classes, the teachers just covered the basics. I learned the parts of speech and how to write complete sentences and short paragraphs, but I never wrote actual essays.

For my college writing class, I received permission from the Office of Disabilities Services (ODS) to use a computer, since it was easier for me to type than to write. However, finding somebody on campus to move a desktop toward a classroom was a hard task. Sometimes I had to push the computer from the computer lab, all the way through the hallway to the classroom. By the time I got to the classroom the class had already started. Occasionally the computer technician or the EOF secretary moved it for me.

During my first semester, I ended up dropping my math class, but I passed grammar with a grade of B- and reading with a B. I was disappointed that I got a D in writing, so I had to take that class again. My counselor suggested I lighten my workload to two only courses starting the following semester.

In the spring of 1998, I repeated the basic math course and enrolled in the next level reading class. I passed both with B-. I also took CIS (Computer Information Systems) in the summer session and passed with a grade of C. The next fall semester, however, was a bad one for me, because out of only two courses, I passed just one of them. This seemed to be my continuing pattern, failing one class and passing the other. I was growing frustrated, because it didn't matter how hard I tried; I was not succeeding in college.

It was very disappointing when my counselor told me to start thinking of a back-up plan. That meant that I should start planning on doing something else instead of continuing in school. She also told me that based on the time I was taking to complete my courses, it would take me 20 years to earn my associate's degree. Usually students attending community colleges full time would complete their program and graduate within two years.

A few semesters later, the situation didn't improve. I kept failing classes, especially the writing class. I grew concerned, because I was receiving financial aid to pay my tuition, but feared I would stop getting it and be suspended from college, because I was not succeeding, The future that I had planned seemed to be vanishing. There were moments when I saw myself as a loser. I thought that I shouldn't keep fighting for something that was not working.

At this point, I hated the English language. I had to learn to write in one way and speak in another. I was frustrated by words that had similar spelling, but different meanings. Past tenses were a nightmare. Most verbs like *cooked, dropped,* and *jumped* have "ed endings" in the past tense, but I had to remember that words such as *arise, become, begin,* and *build* were exceptions.

I was receiving a lot of support from my ESL professors. They tried to find ways to help me. They suggested ways to improve my writing, such as writing every day, going over my mistakes, paying attention to how the letter "s" at the end of a word made that word plural, and working on developing a "thesis" in writing. Although I followed their suggestions, my progress was slow.

When I first started attending college, I spent six to seven hours studying almost every day. I also thought being a part-time student would give me a better chance of succeeding, but that didn't seem to be the case. The CP also affected my learning abilities. My brain took longer to memorize the lessons I needed to learn.

I was the first generation in my family to attend college. Consequently, at home they were unfamiliar with my new routine. My family offered me a lot of support, but they really didn't understand why I had to study for longer hours every night including weekends. I felt overwhelmed.

I was dealing with multiple challenges. Aside from being a first generation college student, I was also coping with a cultural gap, language issues, and a physical disability that caused me to take longer to read, write, eat, shower, get dressed, and so on. I had difficulty managing my schedule, and didn't have anybody around to tell me how to balance college life and personal life.

I did meet regularly with my college counselor and made her aware of the situation. Not passing some courses was a proof that something was wrong. However, her suggestion was to look for other alternatives instead of pursuing my education. That was not the advice I wanted to hear.

Nevertheless, I saw myself as a typical *muchacha*, a girl whose major goal was to earn a college degree. As I was pursuing my dream, I also was breaking down certain barriers. It took a while to learn how to say the word "No" when my family or somebody else asked me to go out with them. Often I wanted to say yes and go out, but I had to take care of my academic responsibilities first. All these issues confused me; I had no idea how to handle the situation.

CHAPTER 8

DEFEATED

It was fall 1998, and academically I wasn't doing much better than before. I was still taking only two courses at a time, and passing one class while failing the other. I turned to Diane Moscaratolo, who was then the coordinator of the ODS, and told her that I needed information about the job market. My grades were not improving, and I faced the possibility of losing my financial aid.

I decided that if the financial aid department stopped covering my college tuition, I would have to get a job and pay for it myself. In my heart, I really did not want to give up my college dream, but I was thinking of what my counselor had said, that I should have a backup plan if college didn't work out for me. I told Diane all my concerns, but I never mentioned the prediction my counselor made about taking 20 years to get my degree.

Diane suggested that the best way to determine if I could meet the academic demands still ahead of me was through a psychological evaluation. I decided to go for it, but how I would pay for it? Diane advised me to contact the Division of Vocational Rehabilitation (DVR) to see if they might help pay for the psychological evaluation. I also wondered if DVR could help with the tuition or with getting me a job if I lost my aid and had to pay tuition myself.

I contacted DVR in December and several weeks later, after I completed all the paperwork, I became a DVR client. It was now mid-spring 1999, and I was struggling with my writing class. When I learned DVR would pay for a psychological evaluation, I decided to do it and see if I was really capable of the academic demands of college.

The evaluation was held in early June at the DVR office in Paterson and consisted mostly of questions to determine my IQ level. At the end of the month, I met with the psychologist, Dr. Lorenzo Puertas, to find out the results. They were discouraging. Dr. Puertas said my IQ was low average for a person of 26 years old, my age at the time. He explained the scores of my test and what each number really meant and told me that the CP was affecting my ability to learn.

I had hoped for better news that would have kept me motivated to continue college. This was the first time since I moved from the DR that I really felt a strong sense of being different from the rest of my classmates and from people of my own age. I saw myself diminished compared to the others.

But Dr. Puertas said something that had a significant impact on me as a student. He said, "Nobody can take away from you the right to get educated." He then gave me the phone number of a legal firm that specialized in education. His words were a sign not to give up.

The next day, I stopped by to tell Diane about the evaluation results. She also encouraged me to keep pursuing my education, but there was still the issue about losing my financial aid. The DVR would help with tuition, but only if I attended college full-time. "I am struggling with only one class a semester," I thought. "Attending full-time would be a disaster." If I got a job, I might be able to pay part of the tuition, but I couldn't afford to pay all of it for as long as it might take me to complete college.

In the meantime, my parents and brothers continued to support me, by driving me back and forth to college. I admit I was disorganized; I didn't plan ahead. Sometimes I told Mami to pick me up at a certain time and I came out an hour later. I stayed longer talking with the professors about the issues I was dealing with or finishing an assignment at the lab. Cell phones were not common then, so it was hard to notify Mami if I was delayed.

In the spring of 2000, after failing Advanced Writing ESL (third level) for two consecutive semesters, I made a very difficult decision. I dropped out of college. My biggest dream of earning a degree seemed to die. When I found out that I didn't pass the course again, I felt so disappointed I could not continue and did not know what to do next.

Negative Evaluation

After a couple of phone calls with my former counselor from DVR the conclusion was to undergo a Vocational Assessment evaluation at Kessler Institute for Rehabilitation, a major facility in West Orange, New Jersey. The assessment was conducted by a guidance counselor, Marybeth Haughey, and consisted of a few hours of testing over the course of a couple of days. My family took turns driving me back and forth.

The final report was very complete. It included a brief summary of my physical condition, a description of the different types of tests that I took during the assessment, and my educational history, including the CP Center, high school, and the courses I took at PCCC. The report also mentioned my volunteer work experience at the CP Center. In addition, Marybeth listed my hobbies, including writing and reading and included details from our conversation about my interests and what type of job I might enjoy.

One of the recommendations made in the report was to seek supported employment. With the help of a job coach, I could work as a file clerk where my duties would include faxing, filing, photocopying and some computer work. Phone coverage was also possible, but not for long periods due to my speech impairment. This would be a first step to strengthen my job skills.

I thought these recommendations were very realistic and that I would enjoy doing that type of work. After the new evaluation, I felt a little more optimistic, but in my heart, the desire to go back to college was like a flame that had become too strong to extinguish.

Based on the evaluation results from Kessler I started looking for a job or a short certificate training program. I wanted to find some type of work in computer data, as a receptionist or file clerk. I was also interested in working with children who had disabilities. I wanted to get the training necessary to get a job and feel accomplished as a person.

I had kept some brochures and pamphlets from different events that I attended for people with disabilities. The brochures were from various agencies and I called the ones with advocacy services in hopes that I could get some job training and employment assistance. Some phone numbers were disconnected or changed. When I did reach someone, he or she had a hard time understanding what I was saying over the phone, due to my speech. So it was a little challenging, but I managed to explain what I wanted and asked them to mail me information about their services.

Every week, a yellow or a white envelope arrived in my mailbox with information from organizations and agencies throughout North Jersey. Unfortunately, all my research turned up negative results. Physically there was not that much that I could do to qualify for some jobs. Academically, I was not ready. Plus, my English skills were still weak.

A few months later, I found out about a file clerk certificate program that seemed to offer the type of training I was looking for. For most people, the training and the job seemed to be a piece of cake, but not for me. I would be required to undergo a series of evaluations to see if I qualified for the training. Unfortunately, I couldn't afford the evaluations or the training.

I sought funding from DVR, but the department refused to pay for both. It was a vicious cycle. A counselor said that since I dropped out of college there was no guarantee that I would meet the requirements to take the job training. Finally, after I persisted over and over, the agency agreed to pay for the evaluations, training, and transportation.

So, in the fall of 2000, I participated in yet another evaluation. This was a two-week assessment in order to determine if I would be capable of completing successfully the Clerical/Word Processing Skills Training Program. The assessment was conducted by a job coach and a career counselor at West Essex Rehabilitation Center (WERC), in Montclair, New Jersey.

By then, I was 28 years old. This time the results of the new evaluation were very different from my previous one at Kessler. They portrayed a person I didn't recognize. WERC's evaluation only briefly pointed out my strengths in literature and my above average potential in music, drama, protective service, and social service.

However, my weaknesses were highly emphasized and the report focused on my physical limitations from CP and my learning disabilities. Based on the results, I lacked realistic and clear vocational objectives, had little awareness of job requirements, and showed a high level of distractibility. My academic levels were judged to be grade 4 in reading and math, grade 6 in spelling, and below average in reading comprehension.

The results indicated that I had difficulties retaining sequences of steps on multiple tasks, limited ability to comprehend, and difficulties accepting constructive criticism. I was considered unable to take initiative, or to follow directions appropriately. I was labeled socially, emotionally, and vocationally immature, an evaluation that left me with a very negative image of myself and of my future options.

WERC offered a variety of services including job searches, training, and placement for people with disabilities, but based on the evaluation, I didn't qualify for their job training. However, they suggested I join their workshop that employed people with disabilities to gain experience. I decided to do it, but found it very frustrating. I worked 12 to 21 hours every week at a long table, sitting in line next to other workers. I packed endless cartons with plastic combs, soaps, and travel kits and was paid less than minimum wage.

This was not what I had dreamed of for myself. When I started working at WERC, I lied to myself pretending that I liked the job in order to cope with the situation. The truth was that I didn't like working on an assembly line, I didn't like packing, and the unfair wage was ridiculous to the point of being an abuse. Even though the job didn't require physical work or schooling, I did the work to the best of my ability.

Since I was a new worker and took my responsibility seriously, I expected a fair pay. Paychecks were handed out Friday afternoons by a supervisor. When I opened the white envelope and saw the check amount, I would be upset. For working 21 hours, I received $37.65. Another week I worked 19 hours and got paid $15.50. Getting up in the morning to go to work there made me very unhappy. I tried asking for a better job at WERC, but nobody helped me.

I wanted to quit, but what would I do? Just sit at home and watch TV? After a year, I quit the workshop. I got tired of not being paid fairly and of not enjoying my job. Becoming well educated was my dream, especially after I tried so hard to earn a high school diploma and even attended college for a while. I realized that my key to succeed was going back to college.

CHAPTER 9

GENDER AND GENERATION GAPS

Even though I had much support from my family, especially from Mami, I had to deal with a gender gap regarding education. Mami has always been a typical *mujer Dominicana*, a married woman and mother in charge of the house and taking care of the family. After Mami arrived in Paterson, a new task was added to her life, getting a paying job.

Mami's mother never worked either until she moved to Paterson. The first job that Abuela had was as a baby-sitter. One of the things that I learned from Mami and Abuela was that a woman's major responsibilities were to take care of the house and be always there for their partners and their children. At that time, most of my aunts and female cousins were married and the single ones were planning to marry someday.

One day, at age 20, before I started high school, I was talking with Abuela Gregoria, who was making dinner, I asked her *"cuales son las cualidades de una buena esposa"* (What are the qualities that a good wife should have?) She told me, *"Para que una mujer pueda casarce ella debe saber lavar, saber planchar muy bien las camisas del esposo, cocinar, atender a los hijos, y mantener la casa limpia.*" (In order for a woman to get married, she should be able to do laundry, iron her husband's shirts nicely, cook, take care of the kids, and clean the house.)

Abuela never mentioned sexuality. In her generation, women were raised to believe that talking about sex, even among other women, was immoral. Women who did talk about it, were seen as *putas*, or whores. Another thing not mentioned is that in the culture I grew up in, a woman's dreams, feelings, and self-care were at the bottom of her priority list

As a young lady now living in America, I viewed the role of a wife differently. To me, Abuela had described the qualities of an excellent maid, whose work is not appreciated most of the time in the DR.

Mami's past experiences had also motivated me to earn a college degree, since her dream of becoming educated never came true. Mami was allowed to attend school only through the fourth grade, although she wanted to keep learning. It wasn't a priority for girls of her generation to become educated. That's why Mami understood my desire to get educated. She could see herself in me and in my ambition to go to college.

After I moved to America, I realized that women can be doctors, police officers, journalists, writers, and just about anything that men can be. I did not plan to be just a wife or a mother, who was always taking care of others first and doing housework. I was living in America and I wanted to act like *las Americanas*, who go to college then start to work in jobs related to the field that interests them.

Sometimes, while I was doing homework, I asked myself, how could I bridge the generation gap if I was Dominicana? I was raised differently. I was expected do what I had learned from past generations. Even though I was in college, my responsibilities went beyond just doing my homework. I also had to help with the housework, do the dishes, and help Mami clean the house on the weekends.

For me as a woman, it was hard to say "I am sorry. I can't do the dishes, because I need extra time to study." I had to learn how to say these words. It was a new language for me and would be harder to master than English.

My Mother's Footprint

Mami played the most important role in my life, and it has shaped who I am as a person and as a woman. As a young girl, I didn't want to live my life the same way that Mami had to live hers, although I admired her because of the way she raised me. I can describe Mami as a clever woman who always tried to maintain a great relationship with me and who built a unique connection between the two of us. She taught me to trust her, to see her as a friend, and to ask her for advice. She always gave me her love and support.

After I moved to America, as my desire for an education increased, so did my desire to end the pattern of women in my family who were denied education. I was touched by Mami's revelation about attending school only to grade four. I wanted to make a change. I realized that back in the

DR, my future was uncertain not only due to CP, but also because of my gender.

I had other reasons for seeking freedom from the role assigned to women in my culture. Since the time I was very young, I heard my female relatives and Mami's friends complaining about their men. I never heard a woman say that she was happy with her marriage. Their complaints were always related to their men cheating on them, lying, and getting drunk. When a group of females gathered together in the kitchen of our home, they sounded as if they were in a support group, expressing their frustration and anger.

Even though I was not allowed to participate in their conversation of *desahogo* (releasing their frustration), from the backyard, I could hear the women telling horrible stories about their relationships. They described their partners as selfish and called them *perros,* a word that literally means dogs, but in this context refers to the worst men. They complained about their *mujeriegos,* men who have a lot of women. All they wanted from their female partners, the women said, was to have sex.

The women described a life of discomfort. By the time men came home from work, the meal had to be ready, the house clean, and their men's shirts ironed nicely. Oh, and after a day of housework, the women had to be ready to please their partners sexually, even if they didn't feel like it.

Some of these couples were not officially married, but married or not, women didn't have the right to complain to their men. It was common to hear female gossip about the guys cheating on their partners. But if a woman was caught cheating on her guy, she was considered a *puta.* People would judge her.

These stories about the horrors of marriage were strong on Mami's side of the family. Some of her sisters and female cousins were in unhealthy relationships. Actually, once my aunts moved to New Jersey, the ones who had left their partners behind were relieved.

In DR, since most women depended financially on their men, they had to accept their situation, because men were *los machos de la casa* (man of the house.) Women obeyed their guys the way pets obey their owners. All these factors influenced my views about marriage and about earning a degree. To me, it didn't make any sense to get married if I would spend the rest of my life suffering for it.

The only exceptions I ever knew to these unhealthy relationships were Mami's parents and Papi's parents. I never heard either of my grandmothers complaining about their spouses. Their marriages lasted for many years, until my grandfathers passed away. But all the other stories that I heard at that stage of my life about unhappy relationships were too powerful for me to ignore.

When I was a teenager, Mami told me that she and Papi were not officially married, although I grew up believing that they were. We lived together as any other family. It just wasn't official. My parents got married years later, when I was around 20 years old.

Hearing all those negative stories made me feel disappointed not only in the idea of marriage, but also about men in general. I was 14 and didn't know what to think about my male relatives. For the first time, I thought of Papi not as my father, but as a man. I wondered if Mami ever experienced what the other women complained about.

Before Papa moved to the US, I remember him coming home from work, eating dinner and leaving the house again. I was told that he was going to a meeting related to his job. He first worked as a cab driver, then he became a driver on a public bus that traveled from Bani to Santo Domingo. Papi was very active in the drivers' union. Even though the union was not strong like those in New Jersey, it was important for Papi to be involved.

The meetings were held in the evenings, but sometimes Papi went out with his friends, too, while Mami stayed home. Did he cheat, like the other men I heard about? Probably yes, he did, but I can't judge him for that, since it was culturally acceptable. Also, he was a good provider. I never heard Mami complaining about the lack of money to buy food or pay the bills, because Papi had it spend it somewhere else. I had always respected their lives as a married couple by keeping my distance from them as spouses.

Since the time I was about 10 years old, Mami warned me not to trust all men. At that time I didn't know why she gave such advice. They way she talked sounded like she was trying to save me from potential harm. She told me to be careful with guys because they can be fresh. Later on, I was able to understand what she meant.

When Mami was a teenager, one of her great-uncles invited her over to his house. He lived in the town, and she didn't know him well, but her parents gave her permission to go. Once she got to his house, Mami found that nobody else was there, just him. Her great-uncle asked her to dance and tried to kiss her. Mami managed to escape and run next door where another great-uncle was living. She asked her aunt-in-law to let her stay. Mami never told her parents what had happened.

This horrible experience had a big impact on the way Mami raised me. She tried to prevent me from being the victim of men like her great-uncle. "Sit up straight. Keep your legs closed, especially if you wear skirts," Mami always told me "If a man seems too friendly *ten cuidado el quiere algo* (he is looking for something in particular). Don't let any man touch you for any reason."

Mami also encouraged me to trust her and let her know if someone tried to touch me in an inappropriate way. Eventually, those words of caution and wisdom helped save me from harm on two different occasions. One morning, when I was 12, I was standing on the porch of our house in the DR. A male neighbor passed and touched my chest. I immediately went inside and told Mami. "Next time that you see him coming, walk inside," Mami told me.

The second incident occurred a few years later, when we were living in Paterson. Mami contacted a repairman to do some work at our home, the first house that my parents owned. I was in the kitchen by the sink. Once the repair was done, Mami went to get the money to pay for the service. Papi was at work. In our community many times people don't contact a company to do these types of jobs. Instead they look for references from people they know, and usually the job is cheaper that way.

While Mami was getting the money, the repairman approached me and asked me to kiss him. I gave him a stern look and moved back. Based on my physical appearance due to the CP, he tried to take advantage. He thought I wouldn't be able to communicate what he was trying to do to me and that I would allow him to kiss me. Once he left, I told Mami what happened. That man never got any more calls from my house.

Her Role Continues

Fortunately, Mami learned how to read. I was amazed by her interest in reading. She enjoyed it very much, even though she never completed her formal education.

To a certain extent, seeing Mami read motivated me to do so, too. In fact, Mami even gave me books to read. The first one was about a little girl's physical development into a young lady. The second was by Pablo Neruda. I was about 16 years old and enjoyed reading Neruda very much even though I didn't understand why back then. Now I do, and realize how meaningful it is that Mami introduced me to a poet who would one day become a great influence on my own writing.

Mami liked reading novels and magazines. One of her favorites was a women's magazine, *Vanidades*. Every month she went to a magazine stand near home to buy romantic novels by Corin Tellado and Bianca. Mami loves short novels with happy endings. I think for her, reading them was a way to escape from reality. She imagines herself as the main character.

Not being able to continue her education has been Mami's biggest frustration. Three years after the family emigrated to New Jersey, she started taking ESL classes three times a week. Mami and I wanted to become US naturalized citizens. To take the test, we had to learn about US history, the government branches, and the Constitution.

Both of us applied together for citizenship. For me it was easier to learn the information needed to answer the test questions, because I was in high school. The classes that Mami took were only in basic English, but she also needed to learn other information for the interview.

The interview was held in Newark, New Jersey, for a half-hour. I was asked the current vice president's name, but didn't know it. I did, however, know Bill Clinton was the president. While I was getting out of the car, it came to my mind to ask Mami the vice-president's name. When I studied for the interview, I never thought to find out the name of Al Gore.

A week later, the naturalization ceremony was held in Newark. On June 30, 1994, I became a naturalized American citizen. I held a little American flag in my right hand, while I was reciting the oath. Two months later Mami did the same.

After she got her citizenship, Mami continued taking ESL classes, offered by the County of Passaic, where we lived. The classroom was located eight steps down in a basement on Smith Street in Paterson. It was a cream-colored room filled with rows of desks. Most of the students were female. The course started out with 20 students, but by the end, only 10 were left.

After a while, Mami decided to stop attending, too, because the lessons were becoming repetitive. She wanted to learn more and researched other education options. She found out about specialized courses for people who hadn't been able to obtain their high school diploma. Mami wanted to take the GED for her high school diploma, but she was struggling in the classroom and felt that getting older had slowed her ability to learn. Mami realized she would need extra study time if she decided to take the GED. But she did not give up.

Her school schedule was convenient. Since she took morning classes, Mami had plenty of time to get home by the time I was dropped off by the school bus. Then, at 5:00 p.m. she left for her part-time job cleaning offices for a big corporation in a town about a half-hour from home.

Mami didn't want to see me in a job like that, so she kept encouraging me to move forward with my ambitions. At the same time, I was seeing my mother trying hard to get an education, but it was challenging for her. At least she tried and that made me proud to be her daughter. I developed a better understanding of why she always supported me and my goals. She didn't want to see me going through the horrible experience of not getting an education.

Juana and Mami

CHAPTER 10

COLLEGE: A SECOND TRY

In January 2002, at age 29, I went back to PCCC. The decision was risky. I knew from experience that the possibility of succeeding was low. But even though I felt insecure about being able to pass all the courses, I realized that education was the key to move ahead in life. I wanted to move ahead, so I returned to college.

Making the decision to return to PCCC meant repeating much of what I did before: Going over the same course material, writing about the same topic, attending lab, trying to take notes the best I could, and studying for tests. When I decided to return, my self-esteem was low, especially after going through evaluations that emphasized my weaknesses.

I had doubts about passing my courses and feared failing again. Yet, I was determined to try a second time to obtain my associate's degree. This time I studied very hard without focusing on passing. Diane from ODS made sure that I would have a computer and a printer available in the classroom, so I would not have to worry about transporting them back and forth.

I took one course, Advanced Writing ESL third level. This was the course I had failed twice before. Throughout the semester, I didn't miss any classes, not even when the weather was bad. At this point, missing any day of class meant falling behind. Also, the professor's attitude toward me and her body language gave me the impression that she didn't like having me as a student. For her, I probably was another student in the class and another paper she had to grade. For me, the class was more than a grade. It was about my future. Regardless of the professor's attitude, I kept proving to her that I was in class because I wanted to learn.

On the final essay I scored a "7" which was considered discretionary. I was between passing and failing, and it was up to the professor to decide. I was anxious, but the third time was the charm. Finally, I passed Advanced Writing ESL, third level.

That summer, I met weekly with a tutor in the ESL lab to work on improving my writing skills. Even though my skills were still weak, my tutor was very impressed with the content of my essays, particularly the essay I wrote in the third week of tutoring. It was about my experience as an immigrant.

Though I had previously received positive feedback from tutors, I never told anybody until that day. When the tutoring session ended, I went to see Diane. Her office was across from the ESL lab. I told her about the positive reactions I received from my tutors about my writing. Diane listened, then asked me to follow her toward the writing lab, which was around the corner. She went straight to the back of the lab, while I sat and waited.

I knew she was talking with somebody about me, but I didn't know who this person was or what the conversation was about. A few minutes later, she returned with Mark

Hillringhouse, the director of the writing/reading lab. He was also an English professor at PCCC and a published poet. I recalled seeing Professor Hillringhouse in the writing lab when I was there for tutoring, but I hadn't met him.

Professor Hillringhouse had a cup of coffee in one hand and a note pad and pen in the other. He had a very pleasant manner and sat down at the same table where I was sitting. He started talking to me about poetry, using terms such as lines, metaphor, and stanza. It was my first time hearing these terms and it all sounded too complex for me. I thought I was in the wrong place with the wrong person.

Then he handed me a piece of paper and a pen and asked me to write a list of words. He gave no other instruction. I wrote whatever cane to my mind: Blue, ocean, birds, sun. When Professor Hillringhouse looked at my list, he said,"Wow!" It was obvious to me that he was impressed, but I didn't understand why. To me the words weren't extraordinary. I come from the Caribbean, and it was natural to have those images in my mind.

Next, he gave me a second sheet of paper and asked me to write 50 words and to come back the following week. He also asked me to bring the writing that I had done in class, and any other writing that I had done in my free time.

At our second meeting, Professor Hillringhouse reviewed my list of 50 words and, once again, was impressed. I still didn't understand why he reacted the way he did. Two weeks later, we met again and went over my new words. Right before I was about to leave, the professor handed me a bag. Inside was a book of selected poems by Pablo Neruda. I was astonished and didn't realize it was a gift. I expected to pay for the book and asked the price, but the professor told me not to worry about it.

Receiving the gift of a book from someone that I knew for only a couple of weeks was something very special for me. It was also meaningful that Professor Hillringhouse gave me a Neruda book, just as Mami had done years earlier.

Despite not understanding why the professor kept asking me to return with a new list of words, I enjoyed writing them. The next time we met was in October, a few days before the midterm exams. This time Professor Hillringhouse's main concern was that I would do well academically, but I ignored that. When he asked me "How are you doing in class?" I said I was doing ok, but it wasn't true. I was getting low grades.

That fall I was taking just one class, and it was the final writing course in the ESL program. Professor Hillringhouse said "If you need help with something, let me know. I am willing to help you." Though he had been nice to me, I still wondered why he seemed to care if I got good grades. After all I went through, I didn't believe in people.

In December when I found out that I failed the course, I worried that I would repeat the same pattern as before of failing and re-taking course after course. The next semester, I had to repeat that course, but I learned my lesson. From that point on, I asked Professor Hillringhouse for advice.

He gave me helpful tips to succeed in my courses. His first suggestion was to study for tests ahead of time instead of waiting until the night before. If I got a low score. he recommended going over the test and becoming aware of the mistakes I made. Professor Hillringhouse also suggested that I request a meeting with my instructor, if there was something that I didn't understand, and to ask him or her to explain it. If I had any concerns related to a class, I should discuss those during the meeting, as well.

I continued to go to Professor Hillringhouse regularly for mentoring. One of the exercises he gave me required using my senses of smell, sight, touch, taste and hearing. At home I walked around holding a pen and a notebook. I made a list of the items that I was seeing: Table, chair, photographs from my childhood hanging on the walls, etc.

I also added the smell of rice and beans coming from the kitchen. Mami looked at me as if I were losing my mind. I explained to her what I was doing, and she just shook her head with a smile, while I kept adding things onto the list. The purpose of this exercise was to make me practice observation and apply my imagination.

The following semester, I came to Professor Hillringhouse's office each week with a new draft of my latest poem. The first works I created were called goofy poems. The professor had instructed me to begin a rough draft by imagining an unusual scene. Winter came to mind and in my scene, it was snowing inside my home. He found the final draft outstanding.

> *The house is covered with snow. "Now I have*
> *To wait for the summer to clean this mess."*
> *The furniture, and the food, we can't even eat*
> *Regular meals we have to eat snow instead.*
> *My house is now located in the North Pole.*
> *My daily life routine changed. I wear a coat,*
> *Gloves and boots to sleep. I have to make*
> *My own snow bed.*

That semester I passed the course that I had failed before, Writing 107 in the ESL program. By summer 2003, I was doing great in terms of poetry. As a result, I decided to enroll in Introduction to Creative Writing, which included poetry.

Before I dropped out of college, I had wanted to become a social worker. Since I had faced numerous obstacles because of my disability, I had the desire to help other people in similar situations. I thought my best career option was to work in the human services field. Now that I was doing well in writing, I was confused. I didn't know if I should continue in the human services major or choose a new one. I was aware that the average college student changes majors three times, but I found it confusing. I wished somebody could help me, but I didn't know who I should ask.

I don't believe in coincidence; I think everything happens for a reason. It was mid-May, the spring semester had just ended, and I had to register for the fall semester. I went to PCCC's Center for Student Success and scheduled an appointment with an advisor. I didn't know who my new advisor would be, and I didn't have any particular name in mind to request. I just arrived on time, took a seat, and waited to be called. A few minutes later, I was pleasantly surprised. I was called to meet with Mr. Edward Casey

I didn't know Mr. Casey, but I often saw him walking in and out of the Center for Student Success. Sometimes, while I was waiting for my ride at the end of the day, he passed by and said, "Have a good evening," in a friendly manner, but we never had a conversation. When Mr. Casey asked me what I was majoring in, I told him I was in human services but wasn't sure if I really wanted to stay with that major, because I was enjoying the writing. I also told him about my mentoring sessions with Professor Hillringhouse.

Mr. Casey suggested I undergo an occupational evaluation or career inventory. After going through so many evaluations before, I didn't want any more, but he said it was the best way to determine my strengths and weaknesses for potential career options. I agreed and he scheduled an appointment for the evaluation at William Paterson University, which was nearby, since PCCC did not offer that service.

The evaluation had several sets of multiple choice questions related to literature, language, math, science, art, and other subject areas typically offered in education. The questions and possible answers were displayed on the computer screen, and I clicked the answers I thought were correct. The results were mailed to Mr. Casey at PCCC, and I returned for another meeting to discuss them.

To my surprise, the evaluation showed that my strong skills were in literature, language, and art. Math and science were my weaknesses. It was very precise. That same day, I registered for next semester, choosing courses in creative writing and basic composition. This time, an evaluation had revived, not destroyed, my dream.

The main focus of this creative writing course was to create poetry by using imagination. I enjoyed the class more than I thought I would. Also, since it was an online course, my disability was invisible to my classmates. Sometimes when I didn't understand the material, I would ask Professor Hillringhouse for help, and he carefully explained it. I passed creative writing with a grade of B.

The same semester I took Composition 101, a class that required intensive writing. For the first time, I had to do a class presentation about my project. I had to stand up in front of the class and speak. I was very nervous. I remember the professor sitting all the way in the back with her thumb up, showing her support as I talked about my project. The topic was immigration.

It was also my first time doing a ten-page project. I earned a B+ in this class.

The professor was very encouraging throughout the semester, but when the course was over, I didn't see her again. She was a part-time professor and probably got another job, but I wish I had the chance to see her again because she was a good professor and had a nice personality. I appreciated her and was very proud of my achievement that semester.

Silk City

It was the winter of 2004, when Professor Hillringhouse invited me to join *Silk City Journal*, a school literary magazine. He was one of the faculty advisers. This was my first time being part of a student club. Students throughout the PCCC campuses were encouraged to submit literary work for possible publication in the journal. During the middle of the spring semester, I met weekly with the other club members to discuss the works that had been submitted.

The meetings took place over the course of two months. The club members and advisers would gather around a large table at the back of the library, pass around the submissions and share our thoughts on the poems, drawings, essays and photographs. Then we selected the ones to be published in the next issue. After a while, I became one of the editors of *Silk City.*

In the beginning, I felt a little nervous about participating, because this was my first time joining a club. I had the idea that we were expected to be at a professional level, as if we were working in an actual publishing company. Then I realized that I was wrong. My classmates and I were participating in a learning experience. We were there to learn how literary magazines are created and to gain knowledge outside of the classroom setting.

Silk City Journal was published at the end of each spring semester, and we club members were also eligible to submit work. My first published works were a couple of poems translated from Spanish into English. The original poets were from the DR. With the support of Professor Hillringhouse, I learned how to translate them.

Since Professor Hillringhouse was American, I expected him to ask me to read American poetry. Instead, I was encouraged to read works by a major Dominican poet, Pedro Mir. I told Papi that I needed a copy of Mir's book. Papi asked one of his cousins who was visiting the DR to bring me a copy of Mir's book *Ahy Un Pais En El Mundo* (There Is A Country In The World). I knew very little about Mir and was surprised when Professor Hillringhouse encouraged me to read his works.

After I became familiar with Mir's poetry, Professor Hillringhouse challenged me to choose a poem and translate it. I was shocked, but willing to take the challenge. I chose to translate *Abulia* (Apathy) from Spanish to English. At home, I kept three different dictionaries by the computer, one in English, a second one in Spanish, and a third one in both languages.

The professor gave me specific instructions for how to do the translations: First, type the poem out; second, number each line of the poem; third, go online and search for a website that offers translations for free; fourth, copy and paste the text. Since the work was used for academic purposes, I didn't have to worry about copyrights. Also, online translations often are not completely reliable, so I would have to draw on my knowledge of Spanish to clarify them.

Professor Hillringhouse also introduced me to snapshots, brief poetic reflections. The snapshots I wrote were based on memories from the past that contain vivid images. Later I translated them to Spanish:

<u>Gone</u>

When the sunset and the roses fall asleep
Please don't cry. I will still be here seeing
How the light breeze touches your body.

Cuando la puesta del sol y las rosas duerman
Por favor no llores. Desde aquí veré
Como la suave brisa acaricia tú cuerpo.

After a while, Professor Hillringhouse encouraged me to write essays related to my personal life. I wrote about my experiences as an immigrant, about spending four years without seeing my father, about living with CP, and about lacking formal education. At first, writing in depth about personal experiences was hard, because it brought back memories that I wanted to keep secret. The most painful ones to recall and write about were related to my physical appearance, especially when I was little and the other children ridiculed me.

I was never physically hurt, but their words were painful. Most of the time, the bullying occurred while I was standing in front of my house by myself, and the kids passed by and stuck out their tongues or made fun of me by mocking the way I walked. I would go back inside the house, but I never told anybody what happened. At night, when I went to bed, I would ask why I was born with CP, and my pillow would get wet with tears.

I also wrote about the strangers who would ask my parents why I walked and talked the way I did, all while I was standing right there. Then, the strangers looked at me with pity, saying: *pobrecita,* poor thing.

As I sat in front of the computer, at home in Paterson, my writing took me back in time. While typing, all those emotions that I had kept secret, came to the surface, and I had the courage to let them all out. I was following Professor Hillringhouse's instructions by first describing a situation, then explaining how I felt about it at the time.

I wrote about how disconnected I felt from Papi when I first moved from the DR, and about the pain I felt over my paternal grandfather's death. Moving to a new country and attending school for the first time had a big influence on my writing. It was fascinating to realize, as I was recalling all these memories, how much my life had changed since I was a little girl.

But the accomplishment that I was making in terms of writing didn't happen overnight; it was a long-term process for several reasons. First, my self-esteem was low. I had been so discouraged by some people the first time I tried to make it through college, that when Professor Hillringhouse seemed impressed with my writing, I wasn't sure if he really liked my work or was just trying to make me feel better. Second, there were times when I thought it was cruel to write about such dire moments in my life.

However, my attitude changed when Professor Hillringhouse showed me some of his own poems, which were related to his life as a young man years ago. He was a few years younger than Papi. I was touched by the way he opened himself up through his poetry, especially since in my culture, it wasn't common to hear a man express his feelings. One of the professor's poems that caught my attention was *Route 80*.

Route 80
By Mark Hillringhouse

I have had to wait all my life to learn the simplest things.
I have had to learn how to navigate between my dreams
and what I wake to driving out alone long Route 80
to an unwashed city in the rain.
I have had to learn not to burn like a moth against the glass,
knowing how my father got his Prussian
anger from his from father,
or how not to suffer loss, that I would fail like my mother
into grim sadness.

And strange that I would think of her after all these years,
the earth smell from the Hackensack Meadowlands
bringing me back to her dark eyes and long black air
that autumn we smelled the rain
mixing with the rotting reeds,
the first woman that I would love-
half French, half Vietnamese,
who left me for a soccer player from Brazil.
We parted one spring morning in Iowa. I remember
driving Route 80 all the way from Indiana seven hours
through Des Moines to get to that mid-western college town,
because I wanted to kill her and disappear; because
she was to make her life, which was only just beginning,
in Rio Janeiro.

And as I pull out behind a semi-trailer and speed up,
I wonder what became of her, thinking
she might not even be alive
as I head to work this morning under a low gray sky,
between the wiper's intermittent strokes,
the road disappear slogging with the mist of slow trucks
as I tune a station on the radio,
between the rising octaves of the cellos and the violins,
their heavenly pull of sounds
that feel more like fields of clouds
than a distant continent of firm land.

I had read works by other male poets, but this experience
was different, because I actually knew the poet as a person,
not just through his metaphors and imagery.

There were some real life experiences that I never revealed to anyone, until I started creating poems. I realized it was much easier to express myself through poetry rather than verbal communication. At that moment, I understood that writing became a form of therapy for me to start healing my turmoil from the past.

Cerebral Palsy

I learned how to ignore others who laughed.
"Mama, yo no quiere ser una carga"
I would say to myself.
"Papi, yo no quiere ser un extraterrestre"
I never wanted my parents to suffer
Because of me. I wanted love
Not sorrow. My body curves
Like a sea creature.
My legs bend behind me, my mouth
Always opens in the shape of the letter O.
I am a toddler slower than a turtle.
I am a clown the kids on the street always laugh at,
But I could never laugh at myself.

Despite the improvement I was making as a writer and as a poet, I was still having difficulties with some courses. Math was my hardest subject. I needed to take one more math course and had the option to take mathematics or basic statistics. I decided on the latter, believing it would be less difficult, but I was wrong.

So in the fall of 2005, I enrolled in basic statistics. For this course I had to learn about analysis, data, interpretation, and all the fundamentals related to this field. I didn't enroll in any other classes, because I needed to focus just on this course. Despite the long hours that I spent studying, the course became a nightmare. I was having a hard time completing the assignments. I stayed in the math lab for hours trying to understand how to interpret different types of charts.

Tutors were available in the math lab, but they just spent a few minutes answering my questions. I needed more help in order to have a better understanding of the material covered in class. Though I had the option of dropping the course, I tried to avoid that, since it was the only class I was taking that semester.

One night while trying to study, I felt very frustrated and wanted to throw my textbook out the bedroom window. I had felt this way before I dropped out of college a couple of years earlier. After a while, I put the textbook away and went to bed. The next day I was able to think more clearly. I went to the EOF lab that offered one-on-one tutoring. One of the tutors there gave me the kind of help I needed by explaining step-by-step the course material I needed to understand. I continued to go there for the rest of the semester for tutoring.

At that time, grade reports were sent to students by regular mail. I was anxious to find out my grade, but I had to wait for a couple of weeks. Finally, it arrived. My final grade for Basic Statistics was a D. I wished I had received a higher grade, but at least I didn't have to repeat the course.

Now, my fear of not succeeding in college returned. There were many courses I still had to take to earn my degree? Would I ever make it? I went to see Professor

Hillringhouse at his new office in the campus library. By then I had a good relationship with him, and I expressed all my concerns. I felt relieved to have somebody I could count on. In the past, I didn't get the support that I needed. Now I had someone on my side. He encouraged me to stay in college and keep working hard. He felt that I could make it.

The professor's words of encouragement made me feel powerful. He believed in my potential as a student and that made a big difference. Every time we met, Professor Hillringhouse asked how I was doing in my classes, and if I had taken any tests recently. His concern regarding my academic status meant a lot to me.

In fact, Professor Hillringhouse became my major source of emotional support outside my family. In college, he was the person I trusted most when things didn't go the way I wanted.

The following semester, I signed up for Introduction to Sociology and Hispanic American Literature. Both courses required a lot of reading and memorization, and Professor Hillringhouse motivated me to keep reading in order to strengthen my reading skills. On weekends I stayed home, sitting at a small table in my room, reading and going over class notes. When I felt the need to put the textbooks aside and take a break, I would stand by the window and gaze at the scenes outside.

In mid-April when the weather started to grow warmer, I saw people walking, wearing light clothes, enjoying the sunshine and pleasant weather. Though I longed to join them, I chose to stay inside, studying for the final exams that were fast approaching. By then, I started to feel more confident about myself. I had the inner strength to say "No; I can't go out, because I have to study."

My family supported my decision, although often I wanted to close my books and go to the park with them. At the end of the semester, I received my reward for staying home and studying. I earned an A in both Intro to Sociology and Hispanic American Literature.

Many of my classmates were enrolling in summer classes. Some of them eventually graduated earlier as a result. I asked myself, "When will I get my degree? How long will it take me? Summer classes met four days in a row for six weeks. If I attended, I would not have enough time to do homework for the next day's class, since it took me longer to complete assignments. This was not a problem during the fall and spring semesters, because I was able to schedule my classes with a day off in between.

In the meantime, I continued to meet with Professor Hillringhouse throughout the summer. In addition to writing essays, creating poetry, and doing translations, I also was learning how to write haiku, a form of poetry that originated in Japan and has a unique structure.

Professor Hillringhouse gave me two books of haiku translated into English. I loved creating my own haiku and often chose nature or my life experiences as subjects. I wrote the poems in English, then translated them into Spanish.

This rain
Symbol of my sadness
Road with no end

Esta lluvia símbolo
De mi tristeza
Camino sin final

One day I asked Professor Hillringhouse why the evaluations I had been given in the past, when I dropped out of college, pointed out all my weaknesses instead of my strengths. "They didn't evaluate your creativity skills," he replied. That answer lifted my spirits.

In the fall, I registered for two courses, Political Science and Environmental Science, but by mid-semester, I dropped Environmental Science, because I failed the first two tests. Political Science wasn't an easy course for me, either. The course objective was to learn about diverse types of government around the world during different time periods. Part of the class requirement was to discuss the topics and express our opinions.

I tried to record the lecture with a tape recorder that I was allowed to bring into class, but after a while I realized that recording while the professor was lecturing was disturbing some of the other students, so I stopped. I tried my best to take good notes and pay careful attention to the lecture. The reading material was much more difficult to understand and memorize than the material I studied in previous courses.

Not using the tape recorder made the class even more challenging for me. My commuting problems also complicated matters. I had to depend on one of my brothers to take me to school and pick me up. Back in 2003, I tried to apply for Access Link (AL), a public transportation service for people with disabilities. The first time I applied, the service was denied, because I lived within walking distance of a bus stop. I had the right to appeal that decision and provide additional documentation showing that I was unable to take public transportation due to my physical limitations.

The next day I called my former case manager, Michael Jackson, from the Division of Developmental Disabilities (DDD), a state agency that provides several types of services, including advocacy. Michael wrote a letter on my behalf explaining why, with my particular disabilities, it would be unsafe for me to use public transportation, especially during bad weather. It worked. This time I qualified for the service and also learned an important lesson about fighting for my rights.

It was October and midterms were right around the corner. The temperature was in the low 50s. While I was sitting on the bench waiting for my ride, I noticed how the leaves on the trees were changing colors, falling, and covering the ground in gold, brown, and red. As I watched them, I felt that each fallen leaf symbolized every test that I had failed since 1997.

It was already autumn of 2006, and I was still trying to get my associate's degree. I sensed the need to change, just as the landscape was changing with the season, but I also sensed that I could not rush this change. It would happen, as in nature, when the time was right.

In the meantime, I continued to work hard in my Political Science class and tried to raise my grade to a "B," but it wasn't possible. The final grade was "C." I was now in my mid-30s. Graduation seasons came and went, while I remained at PCCC, taking one course per semester. I thought it was time to take a risk.

I decided to challenge myself by taking two courses instead of one, so in the spring 2007 term, I registered once again for Environmental Science and also for Introduction to Psychology. Both courses required a lot of reading and memorization, but my desire to graduate was becoming stronger as the semesters came and went. The only way to graduate sooner was by increasing my course load. I was determined and ready.

The environmental science course focused on ways to protect the environment and was designed for students who were non-science majors. There were two class lectures and one two-hour lab period each week, Much of the reading material involved scientific terms I was not very familiar with, such as atoms, molecules, and pH scale. I also had to learn the basic steps of the scientific method: Posing a hypothesis, doing background research, and testing the hypothesis through a lab experiment. Finally, I showed the results to the professor.

In lab sessions, I conducted simple experiments by applying the concepts covered in lectures. Test questions were based on material from both lectures and labs. It was very demanding for all of us.

When classmates asked if I had a paid job, and my response was, "No," they said, "That's good, because you have plenty of time to study." What they didn't know was that for me, attending college was like having a real job, because I took so much longer to study.

In addition to the weekly lectures and labs, I also had tutoring sessions. Every Monday I met for an hour with a tutor from the science department. Usually, we would review that week's reading assignment. We had to read a chapter per week, and the chapters were long, with many illustrations and explanations. At home, while I was reading the assignment, I highlighted everything in the textbook that I didn't understand and asked my tutor to explain the material the next time we met.

While I was working so hard, I was also discovering that attending college offered me an education beyond academic knowledge, but some of what I learned was disheartening. Repeating the Environmental Science course opened my eyes to some sad realities about schools and how they sometimes fail people who are poor, have disabilities, or are of certain ethnicities.

Since I didn't receive formal education as a child, my background in sciences was weak. In high school, the only course I took that related to this subject was natural science during my freshman year. It was taught at a lower level under the special education curriculum.

Unfortunately, in a poor city like Paterson, the school system lacked resources, which prevented students from receiving a good education, especially compared with other districts. Some teachers showed little interest in helping students. I even recall sitting in classes where no material was taught. Instead, we watched movies that weren't even related to the course.

In high school, I noticed that special ed students were treated differently from students enrolled in regular classes, especially in terms of expectations for higher education. Ethnicity was also a factor here. Some educators and school administrators didn't expect the students from special ed or from the Hispanic community to apply to college.

Therefore, I didn't hear many of my special ed classmates talk about continuing their education after high school graduation. Their goal was to get a paying job. I was one of the few students in that department who planned to attend college, and it was in big part due to the support of Ms. Valentin, who assisted me in classes and of my health teacher, Dr. Lugo. Otherwise I probably wouldn't have applied for college.

At PCCC, having a weak background in science made things even more difficult for me. While I was taking environmental science, I sometimes studied until 1:00.a.m. It wasn't too bad when I didn't have class the next morning and could sleep late, but it was very hard when I had an early class the next day or when there was a test coming up.

Mami would knock at the door and see me with the textbook in my hands. She would walk toward me, give me a kiss, and whisper, "Juana, put the book away. Go to sleep, it is late."

As a student with a disability, I was legally allowed extra time to complete tests. One day, while I was taking the first test for the science class, I worried that the other students, who are not allowed extra time, might think I had an advantage.

Did my professors think so, too, I wondered? After all, this was college, not special education. Later on, I expressed my concerns to Diane. She told me there was nothing to worry about, because I didn't have any privilege. The extra time allowance was granted by the Americans with Disabilities Act and was based on the fact that I needed more time than students without a disability to process information. Diane's explanation made me feel better.

I also devoted a lot of time to studying for the Intro to Psychology class. The course was interesting and focused on concepts such as personality, memory, sexuality, learning, and gender. I never got bored, but the tests were hard, and there were days when I considered dropping the course. However, this semester, I did not drop either course and passed Intro to Psychology with a C and Environmental Science with C+. That spring, I met the challenge of completing two courses in the same semester. It was a major moment for me!

PCCC is one of the few colleges that still require students to pass a writing exam in order to graduate. I decided to meet this challenge head-on. Before the 2006 fall semester started, I went to the college writing lab and asked a tutor there how to prepare myself for the exam. He directed me to a website that offered online tutoring. That week I started submitting essays online. In less than 24 hours, I would receive feedback from a tutor. I made the necessary corrections and sent the essay back, continuing that process for several more revisions.

My workload now included classes in Psychology and Western Civilization 101, as well as practice for the writing exam. In order to manage my schedule better, I took Intro to Psychology online which gave me more flexibility. Also, a tutor from the EOF lab reviewed my practice essays with me. When we both thought I was ready, I scheduled the date to take the college writing exam. On the day of the exam, I felt confident that I would pass.

The exam required me to write an essay of five paragraphs: an introduction, three body paragraphs, and a conclusion, the same format that I had been practicing. With the approval of the ODS, I was allowed to type the essay, since I had difficulty writing by hand. No other students were taking the exam at the same time, so the test proctor and I were the only people in the testing room.

After I completed the test and submitted it to the proctor, he gave me a form to fill out and asked me to write my name the way that I would like it to appear on my diploma and include the date that I expected to graduate. When I wrote my graduation date on the form, I felt excited. At that moment graduation seemed like a reality, not just a faraway dream.

But my excitement faded when I recalled how much was still left for me to do in order to graduate. A couple of months earlier, I met with my academic advisor, for my college evaluation and learned that I still needed 60 credits to graduate. Though I had met more than half of the requirements, some of the courses I took to raise my skills to college level didn't count toward the degree. I still had to take a few more courses and also pass the writing exam.

The writing exam would be read anonymously by a panel of professors, and I had to wait two weeks for my results. When the envelope finally arrived in the mail, I tore it open, ready to celebrate. What a disappointment! I did not pass. I knew it was not unusual for students to re-take the test, especially students whose first language was not English. Still, I felt crushed. I had been so confident I would pass the exam on my first attempt.

Suddenly graduation seemed distant again. I realized how much more work lay ahead of me. I repeated the whole process again of preparing for and taking the writing test. I wrote practice essays, scheduled a new test date, and waited two weeks for the result. My expectations of passing the test the second time were even higher, because I worked harder.

But once again, I did not pass. The second failure caused me to question myself. Writing was my strength, or so I thought, but was I wrong? Evidently, I needed to work more on my grammar. With final exams for my courses and the Christmas break approaching, I would not have another chance to re-take the writing exam until school resumed in the new year.

So once spring semester started, I went back to the EOF lab for more tutoring. This time I wasn't as optimistic as I had been before. For the third time, I repeated the whole process and waited a long two weeks for the results. This time, when the letter arrived, I was not so confident about what I would see when I opened it.

Slowly, I tore the envelope open, unfolded the paper, and could not believe my eyes. "Dear Juana, Congratulations. You passed the writing exam!" I cheered. Now, I was one graduation requirement closer to my diploma.

EOF Awards

During the winter break, EOF held an annual conference at the college's main campus. Students who were part of the program were required to attend. The day started with breakfast at the cafeteria, registration, and a welcome message by the director of EOF, Michelle Softley, who provided an overview of the conference events.

In her message, Ms. Softley emphasized that we should be thankful for everything that we had received. The best way to show gratitude, she said, was by volunteering. Giving back to the community was a major aspect of EOF and though I did not have the time or strength to volunteer while in college, I recalled the satisfaction I had years before from volunteering at the CP Center.

Then, I looked over the program and chose two workshops I wanted to attend. Each focused on specific topics such as strengthening reading skills, transferring into four-year institutions, internships, careers, and volunteering. After the workshops, we took a lunch break, then gathered for the recognition ceremony where EOF presented awards to students for various reasons.

Over the years, I was recognized several times by EOF. In 1998 I received a "Certificate of Leadership;" In 2005, I was awarded a "Certificate of Achievement," and in 2007 I received the "Spring 2006 Distinguished Scholar Award," because I earned an A in both of my courses Introduction to Sociology and Hispanic American Literature. This was a major accomplishment for me after having a tough semester in the fall of 2005.

Depression: My Other Battle

About that time, I noticed that I had grown moody. There were days when I got annoyed about anything and didn't look to my future with the same optimism as before. Getting out of bed and taking care of my academic responsibilities made no sense. I had become depressed since the previous semester, but it took me a while to become aware of it.

Depression can be hard to detect, especially if the person with depression knows nothing about this condition. In my native culture, depression was a taboo, so nobody talked about it. When I was in high school, I noticed Ms. Valentin reading a book in Spanish related to depression and religious faith. She was Catholic and had strong religious beliefs. The title caught my attention. I became curious about depression and wanted to learn more.

I asked Ms. Valentin to buy me a copy. The book cost $10 and was for sale in her church. It helped me to understand a little more about what I was going through, and helped me to cope with working at the workshop when I did not have much motivation to go to that job.

One morning I woke up feeling so discontented with life that I just wanted to toss my textbooks in a garbage bag and drop out of college. But then I wondered what would happen if I did that? Would the decision be worth it? How long would I be happy with that decision? A day or two? Then what was I going to do?

I was confused. I could not see a positive outcome. I also thought of all those who had believed in me, my parents, my professors, my tutors. I could not betray their trust. After I finished breakfast, I went to my room, slammed the door, and threw on the floor everything that was on top of my dresser. I wanted to vanish and go someplace where nobody knew me.

The short-term solution for how I felt was to grab a bottle of prescription drugs. A while before, my doctor had prescribed sleeping pills for me, because I was having trouble sleeping. So that morning I took one and went to bed. When Mami came back from work at 2:30 p.m. I got out of bed and I told her I needed to see my doctor, because I wasn't feeling well. She called the office and scheduled an appointment for the same day. Since Fridays were one of my days off from school, I didn't miss any class.

At the doctor's office I had the sensation of being in a different body. My bright smile vanished. The doctor asked me what was wrong. Looking down toward the floor for a second, I told him what happened that morning and how I was feeling. He asked me a couple of questions and took some notes. When the appointment ended, the doctor handed me a small piece of blue paper. It was a referral for me to see a psychiatrist and a psychologist.

That was a little shocking, even though I already had the feeling the doctor would suggest that. Mami was sitting in the main lobby waiting for me. On our way home she asked me how it went. All I said was "OK." When we arrived home, Mami went to the kitchen and started preparing dinner. I followed her, grabbed a glass of water, and opened up. I gave Mami more details about the appointment and explained why I needed to see my doctor. Mami looked at me and put a pot on the stove. Then, she walked over to hug me. Her hug calmed my anxiety.

However, I never told her about the suicidal thoughts. I didn't want to scare her with that, since she recently started having some health issues. The main reason I went to the doctor was because of the suicidal thoughts.

On Monday, after I got home from college, I called several places to make an appointment with a mental health professional. All the clinics I called didn't have any appointments available for the next three months. I kept searching until someone suggested I try Barnet Hospital in Paterson. I called and got an appointment for a month later.

This was a hard time for me. Some days, I lost my temper easily, but there were other days when I could control myself. At times, I felt as if a strong wind was blowing inside my mind. I wanted to explode and didn't think I could wait for the appointment. In the meantime, I tried to keep up with my daily routine and continued attending class.

One day after Western Civ class, I headed down to the college cafeteria on the first floor. Once inside, I filled a cup with soda and walked toward the food menu. I chose baked ziti and vegetables on the side. A kind person asked, "Can I help you? Where do you want to sit?" and offered to carry my tray to my table.

The cafeteria had a TV where some students were watching a show. Others talked with friends or worked on their school assignments. I decided to sit by myself and chose a seat near the windows where I had a view of the street.

Across the street from the college was the Paterson Board of Health. As I watched the people going in and coming out of the building, I recalled the first time I went there to get my immunization shots, but was afraid to get up out of the chair to take the ticket with the number. As I was eating my lunch I realized, "Wow, look how far I have come." After lunch, I walked toward the college library, which was also on the first floor near the cafeteria.

I sat at a table all the way in the back, again near a window. Across from the library was an elementary school, and I could see the kids boarding the school buses to go home.

Again, I went back in time and pictured myself as a little girl. But in my daydream, I was going to school like those children. I imagined what it would be like to be in class at age eight. I pictured myself hearing the teacher say "Juana, stop playing and look at the backboard!'

It was mid-winter and the snow of a past winter storm hadn't melted yet. The snow on the ground reminded me of the first day I arrived in Paterson. My biggest dream was to become educated. I also recalled the first time that I visited the college library, where I was now sitting.

I was taking Composition 101. The major assignment for that course was to conduct research and type 10 pages based on the findings. The professor suggested we choose a topic familiar to us, so I chose immigration to the United States, but I didn't know how to start. The professor had encouraged us to ask a librarian for assistance.

Back then, I saw the library as a weird place. That perception vanished as I visited more often. During the semesters that followed, I became more familiar with the library. While I was reading about the earliest civilization for my Western Civ class, I took a moment to reflect about my education and how it had changed me. Now I loved spending time in the library, especially after lunch, with information from the morning lecture still fresh in my mind.

In early March, my visits to a mental health facility near home started. None of my relatives was able to drive me, so I scheduled my ride with Access Link and went on my own. At the entrance was the receptionist behind a small window. When I approached the window, she asked my name and if it was my first time visiting the office. She handed me a form to fill out and asked for my insurance card.

When the paperwork was complete, the receptionist pointed me toward the waiting room. The room was fairly small. There were posters on the wall and a TV was on. One of the posters read *todos necesitamos de alguien quien nos escuche.* (We all need somebody who will listen). That sign caught my attention. At that first appointment, I met with the psychologist, Dr. Luis Dela Cruz who spoke fluent Spanish. I noticed the diplomas hanging on his wall, most from the New Jersey Board of Psychology.

The melody of soft music emanated from the computer. Dr. Dela Cruz sat at his desk, asking me questions and writing as I answered. He asked why I was there. If it was my first time going to a mental health facility, and so on. My first visit was basically to provide information about myself. The second visit would begin the counseling sessions.

Twice a month I met with the Dr. Dela Cruz and once a month with a psychiatrist whom I saw just for 10 minutes. His job was to prescribe my medications and to check how I was doing with them. I took two pills daily, one in the morning for anxiety and a second one at night to help me sleep. The medications were helping me to stay calm during the day, get a good night's sleep, and carry on with my daily schedule.

I liked seeing the psychologist. Every time I walked out of his office I felt less stressed. As time moved on, I opened up more. It was a great feeling because talking with him was like talking with an old, trusted friend. I told him about my childhood, my teen years, my family history, and my struggles to earn my associate's degree. The counseling sessions were key to my recovery from depression. I was in treatment for nearly a year.

In spring 2008, a few weeks before the semester ended, early registration for the following fall term was in progress. I had to register for two courses, one of them Western Civilization 102 which was a requirement. The second course was an elective, and I had the option to choose from a list which course I wanted to take. I chose Introduction to Print Journalism.

Near the exit of the building, there was a stand with copies of the college's student-run newspaper, *Visions*. One sunny afternoon, I grabbed a copy and sat on the bench where I usually waited for my ride. I sat alone, as usual. In college, I had no friends. I just had short conversations with my classmates, but was usually on my own. While I was reading the paper, Juan, a classmate, was sitting across from me and smoking a cigarette. He wrote for the school paper and we had worked together previously, since he was also an editor of *Silk City*.

Juan stood up and walked toward where I was sitting. Then he sat next to me and said "Hi," in a friendly way. I looked at him and said hi back. Then he said, "You would enjoy working for the paper." His words stayed in my mind. I always noticed the advertisements in *Visions*, encouraging students to write for the paper, but I was skeptical about registering for this course. Living with CP made me wonder if this course would be good for me. My ride arrived, and I left, thinking all the way home about Juan's suggestion.

The print journalism class met once a week at 7:00 p.m. The time would be an inconvenience because the class ended at 9:30 p.m. and there was no guarantee that Access Link would pick me up at the time that I requested, due to their rules. The driver might arrive 20 minutes before or 20 minutes after the time I requested. The solution was to have someone from the family give me a ride back home.

In fall 2008, I enrolled in the print journalism course with Professor Christine Redman-Waldeyer. The assignments for the course included interviewing people and covering events. Then based on the information that I gathered and my observations, I wrote articles for *Visions*. My first important assignment was to interview Maria Mazzioti Gillan, a major New Jersey poet. I had met her once during a poetry reading at the college.

Gillan is the director of the Poetry Center at PCCC, which is highly regarded in the poetry world. Once a month, from October through May, poets from around the country were invited to read at the Poetry Center. Gillan had recently won the American Book Award, and I was assigned to interview her about this honor.

The first step was to contact Gillan's secretary by phone and schedule an interview. Since Gillan travels around the country frequently, I had to keep in mind that she might not be available any time soon. Fortunately, she was around that week and was able to meet two days later. Immediately, I began to create a list of possible questions. Since this was my first important interview, I \wasn't sure how to order the questions.

That evening in class, I realized that my classmates were in the same situation. Professor Waldeyer explained how to conduct an interview and how to create a list of possible questions.

In my case, she advised starting off with simple questions for Gillan. Where she was from, how she started, her reaction to the award that she had received recently. I was advised to leave the hard questions for the end. I learned that was the technique of interviewing, to ask easy questions first and help the person who is being interviewed feel comfortable during the session. I also learned to treat the subject in a friendly way, but avoid getting personally involved.

Upon my arrival at the Poetry Center, I was a little nervous, because it was my first major assignment outside of the classroom. Since I was early, I waited in a room near Gillan's office. The building seemed like a museum because it also had an art gallery. Gillan was already in her office. Even though she was expecting me, I introduced myself and told her the reason for the interview. Then, I asked permission to use a tape recorder. She agreed, and the questions began. Later that evening, I played the tape, and typed Gillan's answers into my computer.

I submitted all my articles on time, which was my main concern regarding this course. In the journalism world, deadlines are crucial, and I managed to meet mine. Plus, I wrote a couple of extra articles. I enjoyed the course more than I expected and received an A as my final grade.

The next step was to do an internship. Professor Waldeyer learned of an internship position at the governor's office. The main office was in Trenton, but there was a second office in Newark that I could get to by Access Link. She encouraged me to apply.

Professor Waldeyer helped me to organize a professional portfolio with samples of my work, mostly pieces that had appeared in the school publications *Silk City* and *Visions.* I also included a resume and two letters of reference from professors. Although the internship was an unpaid job, I would gain work experience.

Internship

I worked for the New Jersey Department of the Public Advocate, which was connected to the office of then Governor Jon Corzine. This department was in charge of providing information and various services to New Jersey residents. I worked for five months, from early March to the end of August, averaging 15 to 18 hours weekly. I didn't follow a specific schedule, because part of the work could be completed online. I went into the office to work on-site once or twice a month.

My first task was to update media lists of various ethnic groups as well as groups that included senior citizens, women, religious publications, and veterans. I also updated contact information for colleges and universities in all 21 counties of the state. Revising these required me to verify current names, phone and fax numbers, web sites, email addresses, and physical addresses. Besides doing the internship, I was also taking my last course, Modern Novel & Short Stories, which I passed with an A. This was my final semester at PCCC and it was the busiest one. Graduation was now only a couple of months away.

Awards and Recognition

On April 22, 2009, a month before graduation, I received two awards. The first was the Academic Achievement award from EOF, and the second was the Recognition of Outstanding Merit and Accomplishment award from Who's Who Among Students In American Universities and

Colleges. Then two days before my graduation I received the Persistence and Achievement award on behalf of the English Department.

All the awards I had received so far meant a lot to me. Each represented the struggles, frustrations, and accomplishments I experienced in earning a college degree. The third award was even more special to me, because it was presented by the person who lit my road in the darkness, Professor Hillringhouse. He was always there for me, often encouraging me with words like "Good job, Juana! You can do it. I am so proud."

Back then, Professor Hillringhouse also had to deal with painful moments: His father's death, then his mother's illness and death. Despite these tough situations, he always had an encouraging word for me. Moments before Professor Hillringhouse presented the award to me, I walked toward the stage of the college auditorium. One of the staff members held my right arm and helped me to walk up the steps. I stood by Professor Hillringhouse as he read from his notes.

He described some of the obstacles that I had to deal with in college and told about my passion for writing and perseverance in trying to obtain my degree. He also expressed how moved he was when he saw me struggling to learn a new language. In his speech, Professor Hillringhouse told the audience of the impact that I had made on his life. "She made me a better person," he said.

His words made me feel humble. I was the one who should have said that about him. When he was finished, I got a standing ovation. Tears started from my eyes, and I went speechless. When I walked back to my seat, Mami was sitting next to me and wiping her eyes. She looked up at me and said, "*Él es un ángel que te ha enviado Dios.*" (He is an angel that God has sent you.) Mami, you are right.

Every time I had to deal with an obstacle, Professor Hillringhouse was by my side saying, "Juana, you are getting there. You will make it." He was like a good father who watches over his child's first steps. He watched over mine until I learned how to walk on my own. Sometimes, I think he was more confident that I could achieve my goal of graduating than I was.

College Graduation
May 21, 2009

On graduation day, Papi came home from work around noontime, because he had something to take care of in the house. When he walked through the door, I rushed at him in my excitement. "Oh, my God, today is the day," I told Papi. The ceremony was in the evening, but early that day my parents bought me balloons with the message: "Congratulations. You Made It!" I asked myself, "That's me? I made it?" Papi hung the balloons over the front steps and shot a couple of photos of me next to them. Mami was still at work.

A few minutes later, I got a phone call from a reporter at *The Herald News.* The publication was working on a story about local students who were graduating from college. Somehow they heard about me and wanted to conduct an interview that day.

The reporter, Meredith Mandell, said she would be at my house shortly. She arrived with a pen and notepad, and introduced herself. Her professionalism reminded me of my journalism class. We sat across from each other in the living room. It was a warm spring day, and sunrays shone through the windows as we talked.

Meredith asked questions about my college experience, writing, my family, childhood background and my plans to attend William Paterson University after graduation from PCCC. She also asked me to show her some of the publications in which my work appeared. I handed her a copy of *Silk City*. Meredith flipped to a page with a couple of my haiku. Reading them aloud, she wrote the words in her notepad. One haiku in particular caught her attention:

> *Did you see those butterflies?*
> *I will follow them*
> *From Paterson to Bani!*

In this haiku I honored two places to which I felt deeply connected, the city where I lived since I first moved to New Jersey, and my place of birth in the DR. When the interview was over, Meredith informed me that she would be at the commencement ceremony that evening, along with a photographer from the newspaper, Michael Karas.

The ceremony was to start at 6:00 p.m., but graduates had to be at the college by 4:30. Mami was home from work and wanted to take some photos of me before I left the house, so I put on my cap and gown and again posed alongside the balloons. Then Papi dropped me off at PCCC and returned home until later.

Since I am unable to walk fast, I did not line up with the graduates to walk over to the gym where the ceremony would take place. It was a long walk from the building where they would meet to put their robes on. Instead I waited in an area close to the gym and joined the line when they arrived there. While I was waiting for them, Professor Hillringhouse sat with me. It was very meaningful to have him beside me on the night I finally achieved my goal.

I thought back to the awards ceremony a few days earlier. After Professor Hillringhouse presented me with the persistence award that evening, I handed him a plaque with a poem that I wrote especially for him to show my appreciation for all that he had done for me.

Mentor

In PCCC I got lost.
High education was my horizon.
Singular, plural, verbs, commas
And periods were in the same box.
Suddenly an angel approached.
Gave wings to my imagination
Freedom to my soul by lifting my dark road.
Filled my empty world with metaphors, images,
Languages, haiku and essays.
Thanks to your support and encouragement
I found a meaning in life!

Then, looking at me, he said, "I got a little emotional when reading it." I didn't know what his reaction would be, since I didn't ask anybody to revise the poem for me. I knew it had a couple of grammatical errors, but I wanted it to be a surprise. Despite the errors, I realized I did well to let my mentor know how thankful I was for everything that he had done for me.

A few minutes later, it was time to line up. Professor Hillringhouse went to join the rest of the faculty, while I walked toward the gym, to wait for the other graduates. Once all the graduates and faculty arrived, the door was opened. As I entered, a security guard held my right arm. The gym was full of relatives and friends, all there to cheer the Class of 2009, the largest PCCC graduating class to date.

I couldn't see any of my guests, my parents, Soris, and Dr. Lugo, but I knew for sure they were there supporting me in my big moment. A few years earlier I had asked Dr. Lugo to be my godfather at my confirmation, a Catholic ceremony similar to baptism. He was one of my inspirations to pursue a college education, and I wanted him to share this night with me.

At the ceremony, I sat in the front row. The newspaper photographer was nearby, shooting photos. When Dr. Steven Rose, the college president shouted, "Congratulations, Class of 2009," my excitement took over, and I was screaming aloud. I had at last earned my Associate in Arts Degree in Liberal Arts/English. I made it.

After the ceremony, we stopped at the college parking lot so Mami could take another photo of me wearing the cap and gown. The college hosted a post-ceremony reception for the graduates at the cafeteria, but we didn't attend, because we had other plans instead.

My parents wanted to celebrate my accomplishment, but not by throwing a party. We decided to go out to dinner at La Hacienda, a Mexican restaurant. Our group included my immediate family, a couple of my relatives, and Professor Hillringhouse and his wife, Linda.

I was a little concerned about how we would all communicate. My family spoke mostly Spanish and Professor Hillringhouse and Linda spoke only English. I didn't need to worry. It was an amazing evening, and we all had a lot of fun. We communicated in the language of friendship, talking among us the way that old friends talk when they get together. It was all so wonderful, I thought I was dreaming.

I sat between Professor Hillringhouse and Linda. She was a professor, too, and even though I didn't have the privilege to be in her classes, we became friends. Sometimes when I needed help proofreading my poetry and Professor Hillringhouse was unable to help me, I asked Linda, since she is a poet too. Once dinner was over, we went outside where Mami took some photos of the group. Unfortunately, two days later, all the photos Mami took were accidentally deleted from her camera. All the pictures from the award ceremony and graduation day were gone! Mami and I felt so sad that we would not be able to enjoy these images in the future. To make me feel better, Papi said those memories will last forever in my heart. Papi was right, but I still wanted the photos of that wonderful evening and was consoled by the fact that Soris also took some photos and shared them with me.

The next morning, I was in the kitchen having breakfast and thinking about the happy events of the day before when Mami called me from her job with surprising news. I had made the front page of *The Herald-News*. "What?"

I screamed into the phone. I could not believe it. After the interview with the reporter, I expected the story about me to appear in a small article on the pages with the less important news of the day. Immediately I went upstairs to my computer and checked the newspaper's website. There I was in a page one article, wearing my cap and gown, and expressing my excitement.

On her way home, Mami bought two copies of the newspaper. As soon I heard her coming in, I hurried downstairs. Though I had already read the story online, it was a different experience to see the article in print. Some of my relatives and people who knew me called to let me know that they just seen me in the newspaper. In the evening, my godfather stopped by with a copy under his arm to congratulate me.

The road to my college degree had been at times full of bumps and at other times a smooth path, as I titled one of the articles that I wrote for *Visions*. Many times I felt hopeless and defeated. There were moments when my dream of completing an associate's degree seemed to be falling away from me, the same way the leaves fell from the trees I gazed at that autumn day so many semesters ago.

But the seed of a dream had been planted in my heart and was watered by those who believed in me when I had a hard time believing in myself. Mr. Casey, the counselor who suggested I take a career evaluation, saw me succeeding as a writer. Once, when I showed him one of my essays, published in *Silk City*, he said, "Someday I can say I knew her before she became famous." Mr. Casey retired a couple of years later, but he will always be in my heart.

And, of course, there was Professor Hillringhouse who was always there for me and wrote in graduation card he gave me, "I knew this day was coming." He was right. My springtime had arrived late, but it was finally here, and like a flower in May, I was in full bloom.

On the bench at PCCC where I often waited for my ride.

The award I received from the PCCC English Department

In my favorite work spot at the PCCC library

Celebrating my PCCC graduation with my
mentor, Professor Hillringhouse.

CHAPTER 11

ON MY WAY TO THE B.A.

I always knew, right from the start, that I would pursue a bachelor's degree. I started preparing for that long before I graduated from PCCC. In September 2008, I went for a tour at William Paterson University (WPU) in Wayne, New Jersey. The director from their Office of Disabilities Services, Jacqueline Safont, was in charge of the tour. Since I take time to walk from one place to another, I rode in a scooter provided by the office.

Hobart Hall was one of the buildings Jackie showed me. I noticed the satellite disks outside. "That's the communication building," she said. Back then, I thought of communication as verbal expression, not writing. At that time, I was taking the introduction to print journalism course at PCCC. The semester had just started, so I knew little about the field.

My original plan was to major in English, since I was into writing, but I felt there was a problem with my choice. Most English majors choose to become teachers, or at least, that's what everyone thinks. Although I loved writing and admire teachers, especially those who made a difference in my life, I didn't want to become a teacher. Teaching is a calling, but the same is true for journalists and writers. We are born into it.

Each time I was asked what my major was, I answered English. People asked me if I wanted to become a teacher and my response was "No." When I said I wanted to be a writer, they often looked at me as if I were strange. But I was in love with poetry and personal essays.

Jackie brought me to the Atrium, WPU's home to the English Department, and I met with the assistant chairperson. We went over the catalog and she explained the program and the requirements for English majors. Yet, I wasn't sure if English would be the right choice for me. I had grown to love print journalism, too.

I asked some professors and other people I trusted for their impression about the two universities in the area, WPU and Montclair State University, where I attended the special EOF summer program when I started at PCCC. The feedback I received was that both institutions were good. I decided to apply to WPU first. In March 2009, I filled out the application and chose print journalism as a major, although I was still unsure of that choice. My transcripts from PCCC were sent directly to WPU.

In early April 2009, I received a package in the mail. Inside there was a letter that read, "Dear Juana, Congratulations! You have been accepted at William Paterson University." I was stunned. I couldn't believe I had been accepted. A couple of days later, I received a second letter, "Congratulations and welcome to the Communication Department!"

The transition was smooth. I was invited to attend a few orientation events at WPU. Each was held for different reasons: To get to know the campus more; to meet faculty, students, and staff; to learn about the variety of majors and minors; to familiarize myself with the registration process; to learn about financial aid; etc. It was all so exciting.

Current students participated in the orientation. They described the clubs and organizations on campus and the advantages of getting involved in extracurricular activities.

They also explained how the transfer process worked. Attending these events was important since a four-year institution is different from a community college in some ways. I was also pleased that all the courses I took at PCCC would count at WPU toward my bachelor's degree.

The staff showed how I could use the "Blackboard" online system even if I wouldn't be taking online courses. Sometimes professors asked students to submit assignments through Blackboard while others posted important information about the courses.

By late July, I was already registered, had my student ID, and applied for financial aid.

In the early part of the summer, I met with one of the advisors from the Communication Department who helped me to choose my classes for the fall. Jackie Safont registered me and showed me the steps to the process, so I could do it myself the next time. My main concern, however, was how much of my costs would be covered by financial aid, since I would be attending WPU part-time.

I did not want to apply for a loan, but in order to cover tuition, I had no choice. I was approved for both the loan and for a grant. Although I would have to repay the loan, the grant helped to reduce the amount of debt.

In September, I started attending WPU and took two courses, Media Writing and Survey Communication. Media

Writing was an overview of how to write for newspapers, television, and the Internet. Survey of Communication introduced students to various concentrations within the communication field. Since I was interested in print journalism, one of my first assignments was to find out information about my major. I interviewed both a professor and a senior-year student who was majoring in print journalism.

Recalling what I had learned at PCCC in Dr. Waldeyer's class, I created a list of questions and showed them to my professor, Dr. Casy Lum. He approved the list, and I was ready to get started. I interviewed Corrado Rizzi, who was a senior at that time and also editor-in-chief of *Pioneer Times*, the school newspaper.

During my second semester, I took Advanced Reporting, a course in which students were expected to choose their own topics and write about them. Each student had to write a proposal and submit it to the professor for approval.. Due to my experience with CP, I proposed to research and write about disabilities issues using Kessler Institute, where I had gone for one of my evaluations, as a resource. My advisor, Professor Elizabeth Birge, approved my proposal.

Eager to begin, I contacted Kessler and scheduled an interview with one of the physical therapists. Then I called Access Link and scheduled my bus ride to the facility. Irene, the physical therapist I would be interviewing, came out to the main lobby and introduced herself, asking me to follow her to a small office. As someone who knew what it was like to receive physical therapy, I was now exploring the relationship from the other end. "What is it like to be a physical therapist?" I asked Irene. "What do you do in a typical workday?" When I started typing the article, I was totally convinced that I really was into print journalism.

The second course I took that semester, Media and Society with Professor Lum, explored the power of the media and their influence on society. One of the most important lessons I learned in the class, though, was through an embarrassing experience I had when I was about to give a presentation. My topic was the degree of influence that advertisements have on parents when they are buying products for their children.

I was nervous about the presentation, because the CP affects my speech, and I was concerned that my classmates would not be able to understand everything I planned to say. Dr. Lum suggested that I write down everything that I wanted to say in advance. Then, while I spoke, the written version, including images, would appear on a screen through a projector.

The classroom resembled a movie theater, windowless, dark, and with specially arranged seating. That day I was sitting in the second row and next to me was a wall. The floor had a bump like those in the movie theaters.

When I got up to do my presentation, I forgot about the bump and I hit the wall! Fortunately, I wasn't hurt, but I felt embarrassed. When Dr. Lum asked me if I was ok, I responded "I am fine." Then, I took my place at the front of the room and started the presentation, despite the embarrassment I felt because of the incident.

After the class was over, Dr. Lum approached me, saying he admired me because of the way that I responded to the situation. His words made me feel better. I had learned a lesson about professionalism and was proud of myself.

For one course, I had the opportunity to write for *Pioneer Times*. My assignments required me to cover campus events. This increased my awareness of the issues that affected the world around me. One of the major stories I covered, a film about domestic violence, made a strong impact on me.

The film, *Finding Face*, was about acid violence against women. The main subject of the film was Tat Marina, a survivor of an acid attack in Cambodia. Ms. Marina was present that evening and was introduced to the audience after the presentation was over. See the film and meeting Tat Marina had a big impact on me as a journalism student and as a human being. I realized that even in the 21st century, there are still people whose voices have never been heard. By writing this type of article, I could tell their stories to readers.

Being a photographer is part of being a journalist, but for me, this part presented unique challenges. One of my first assignments for *Pioneer Times* was to go around campus and take photos of people. Since my left hand is weak. I tried to hold the digital camera with one hand. While I was waiting for the camera to get a good angle of the subject and press the shutter, the flash kept turning on by itself. Sometimes without realizing, I took three shots just in a matter of seconds. Some of the photos came out blurry. Others came out with half of the image, so I had to try again. It was a mess, but also a fun experience.

One of my favorite courses, International Media, helped me to realize how fortunate I was to be able to study journalism and how much freedom journalists have in America compared to other parts of the world. Every day journalists in some countries risk their lives trying to expose corruption and unfair treatment toward people. I was impressed by their courage.

For this class, I did research about these issues and the findings were disturbing. Many journalists were kidnapped, killed, or sent to jail because they tried to publish their work. In some countries, women are not even allowed to become journalists.

A semester later, I did a human interest profile of Jason Moussab, a senior at WPU who was a communication major with a concentration in print journalism. Writing about his life was inspiring and personal, because Jason has arthrogryposis. This disorder reduces the mobility of the joints, but that didn't stop Jason from pursuing his education. He was very active around campus, and I could see how Jason's classmates and professors admired and respected him, regardless of his disability.

When I was near the end of completing all the requirements for my concentration in print journalism, I felt that something was missing. I had an associate's degree from PCCC in Liberal Arts with a concentration in English, so I decided I should go for an English minor at WPU. Even though I loved print journalism, I felt incomplete as a student until I minored in English.

In the fall of 2012, I took two English courses, Advanced Creative Writing and Method of Literary Analysis. This semester posed some extra challenges for me, because once a week, the two classes met on the same day. Thursdays were my long days with classes running from 2:00 p.m. to 8:30 p.m. and a little more than a two hour break in between.

During the break, I first went to the food court to buy something to eat, then I walked to the library for some extra studying. I had to try to catch up, because I was falling behind. A few minutes before 6:00, I left the library to get to my second class. Since Thursday was a late night, I skipped the bus and my brother Alfredo picked me up.

For both courses that semester, the ODS paid a student assistant to take notes for me. Most of the time, though, I had to wait for weeks before the office found the right person for the task. The ODS staff was also a big help with textbooks. Like my classmates I got my textbooks from the bookstore, but I also received an alternative book on CD Rom.

Taking these courses, especially the creative writing, was again like going back in time for me. In this case the word "creative" was not related to fiction. The writing was based on individual personal experience. This course was amazing, because I wrote about myself, reliving my life experiences and sharing the stories with the class. I received great feedback from the professor and my classmates.

The following semester I took Creative Non-fiction, a course that combined English and journalism. For the final paper, I interviewed my friend David Roldan, who also has CP. When I wrote the paper, I also incorporated my own experience into the paper.

Capstone-Print Journalism. This was it… the last course I had to take to complete the requirements for my major and obtain my bachelor's degree! I was almost at my next goal. I expected capstone to be a tough course, so I was a little nervous, On the first day of class, Dr. Tina Lesher explained the course requirements and showed some examples of what former students had done as their capstone project. Some had written magazines, others created booklets, and so on.

The capstone project was to be the representation of yourself in the professional world.

As my classmates were discussing what their projects would be about, I decided I should write a book about my own life. I wasn't sure if Dr. Lesher would approve, but she did more than just approve, she actually motivated me to do it. I studied the syllabus which divided the course into three major parts. First, I had to write a short essay describing the topic of my project. The second part consisted of conducting research related to the topic and creating a literature review of the research sources.

For my project, I researched biography. Based on the findings, I created a literature review of 10 pages, which included information about how to write a biography. This step was hard work. I felt overwhelmed, because there are many sources available online and in print, but not all of them are reliable. As a communication major, I had to select my sources with caution.

I decided to seek expert help, and scheduled an appointment with Nancy Weiner, a reference librarian at WPU and the coordinator of the User Education Program. She helped me find the right online sources for my literature review.

The final step in my capstone was to interview several people who know me and ask them questions about their impressions and perceptions of me. I interviewed Mami, Professor Hillringhouse, and Dr. Lugo. Also, on the last day of class, I had to do a five-minute presentation. I received a grade of B- in that class and was now coming to the end of my baccalaureate journey.

Undecided

Back in the fall of 2012, eight months away from graduation, I hadn't yet made any plans about what I would be doing afterwards. The idea to write a memoir hadn't emerged yet. At that time it was hard for me to accept that I had no plan. The country was going through a major economic recession. The unemployment rate was high. News reports repeated over and over how tough it was for recent college graduates to get hired. Even those who were able to get a job often were not working in their chosen field.

If things were that bad for other people, I thought, imagine how much worse they must be for people with disabilities, who have difficulty finding a job even when the economy is strong. Since I did not expect my situation to be an exception, I chose to focus on the "now" instead. At that time, passing the remainder of my courses with decent grades became my immediate goal, but I kept thoughts about what would come after graduation in the back of my mind.

Sometimes, when I was too concerned about the future and moving forward, I looked back, instead, and reminded myself how far I had already come. Back in the DR, I never thought that one day I would have accomplished all that I had up to that point. I graduated from high school, earned my associate's degree, and discovered my talents as a writer. Soon, I would obtain my bachelor of arts degree in communication.

Recognizing how far I had come helped me to keep my perspective, but I was also aware that I had to find something to do after graduating. Working in my field of study as a journalist or writer would be great, and having a job would enable me to support myself financially and pay off my student loan.

Even though I had always been an optimistic person, the current economic recession forced me to be more realistic. How would I find a decent job, even with my college degree, when I didn't have work experience and the unemployment rate was high? Also, I had a physical limitation. Based on my personal experience, I knew how frustrating it can be to have the desire to move ahead in life, while others were assuming that my dreams could never come true

That's when I started thinking of becoming self-employed. Although I gained valuable work experience while I was doing my internship for the state a few years earlier, I realized that I didn't feel comfortable following instructions from others over long periods of time. I decided to focus on an alternative to looking for a typical job.

I felt the need to have a good conversation with someone who would be willing to listen to me and offer advice. So I called my godfather. Dr. Lugo invited me to his home for Sunday dinner with him and his family. We would have our conversation afterwards.

After dinner, my godfather and I settled down for our discussion. We started talking about how I was doing in college. Then, Dr. Lugo asked me what I planned to do after I graduated. This was a tough question, and I didn't have an answer for it. How should I respond? Should I tell him that I had no plans?

At that moment, something inside of me said that I should reveal my dream. I told my godfather that my desire was to help other people who were in situations like mine and struggling to get educated. Immediately, he approved my idea. I was delighted. This was the first time I let someone know about this desire. The idea of writing my memoir hadn't emerged yet.

From that point on, Dr. Lugo and I elaborated on the concept of helping others and how it could become a reality. I had in mind to create a sort of advocacy group in one of the local schools, but that was just a thought. I was in shock, because Dr. Lugo took my idea even further. He suggested establishing a non-profit organization where I would be the person in charge. My title would be founder and CEO. Those two words sounded ambitious and scary to me, but I liked the sound of them and the thought that they described my future role.

The next major steps in this project would be to give a name to the non-profit, write a mission statement, and register with the state. I decided on the name Rainbow of Talent Of New Jersey Inc., because every person with a disability also has a talent, even though society tends to highlight only the disability. The mission of the organization is to help people with disabilities to succeed in college or a trade program and join the workforce. My godfather helped me register my new non-profit, and I was ready to make this dream come true.

CHAPTER 12

TOUGH DECISION

In spring of 2010, Mami and Papi were taking steps to leave the US and return to the DR. Mami was dealing with some health issues and Papi had reached retirement age, so they were thinking of leaving America and returning to spend more time in the DR. By then, we were living in Woodland Park, a town close to Paterson, and I was in my first year at WPU.

As soon as my parents told me their plans, I set out to contact my former case manager, Michael Jackson, from the Division of Developmental Disabilities (DDD). The state agency provides several types of services, including residential placement. I wanted to stay in Paterson and would need a new place to live. Qualifying for residential housing was a huge problem. An applicant had to be on the waiting list, and I wasn't. The list dated back to 1999 and we were in April 2010. In other words, I would have to wait until everyone already on the list was settled before I could find a place to live!

In May, my parents put our house on the market. Mami and Papi had made up their minds. They were returning to the DR, but didn't want to leave until they were sure I had a place to live. I started worrying, because I didn't see any sign that I would find my own place soon. Would I have to give up the idea of staying in New Jersey once my parents left?

One day I got a phone call from Michael, asking me and Mami to go and see an apartment in Hawthorne, a town close to where we were living. The place looked safe, nice, and neat. I also had the opportunity to meet the staff and a couple of the tenants, too. Nobody offered to show me the actual apartment, and I didn't ask to see it either. I was content that I would have a place to live, and that was my main concern. I assumed I would be able to move in before my parents left, but I was wrong. I was disappointed that I couldn't take the apartment right away, because I had to go through a process first. My plans didn't go the way I expected.

In September, our house was sold. My parents paid one month rent for the family to prepare to move out, and I was on the phone every day calling Michael, because I didn't want to leave New Jersey. Since I refused to leave, Mami came up with an idea. Soris and Alfredo were my two closest relatives in New Jersey, so Mami asked Soris if I could stay in her house until the agency found me a place to leave. It was a good idea, since Soris and I were like sisters and got along well. "No problem," Soris agreed. Then Mami asked my brother if he would watch out for me once she and Papi left. Alfredo's response was, "Yeah, mom."

I was relieved. All my accomplishments would be in vain if I had to return to the DR. I knew down there, I wouldn't have the same opportunities. Once I decided to stay in New Jersey, Mami and I faced harsh criticism from some people who argued that she shouldn't leave me behind, because I would never make it without my parents at my side. Mami did not let the criticism affect her. "I felt confident you would be able to make it," she told me one day. But there were others who supported our decision. They told us that although it would be a challenge for me, they felt that in the end I would succeed.

Mami left first, then Papi. The night before Mami departed, we said our goodbyes. For the first time, we would be living far apart from each other. I started crying like a little baby. I felt scared and realized that by the time I woke up the next morning, Mami would be on the airplane, heading miles away from me. Even though I chose to stay behind, I was also afraid of being on my own without Mami around. Already I felt all alone, like a little child who got lost in a crowd and can't find her mother.

The next day I tried to stick to my daily schedule by attending classes at WPU. I also made phone calls to DDD about moving to a supervised apartment soon. But the process took longer than I expected. Even though my situation was now listed as an emergency, since I was no longer living with my parents, I still had to go through a load of paperwork and doctor visits.

Alfredo drove me to all my appointments. I needed a physical, which included blood work, a couple of vaccinations, and the disclosure of my medical history. A physical exam was one of the requirements to qualify for the apartment. I also had to disclose my finances, because there had to be evidence that I couldn't afford to pay a regular rent.

Juana M. Ortiz

On My Own

My big day arrived on December 1, 2010. Alfredo and Michael helped me move all my personal belongings to a supervised furnished apartment in Hawthorne, near my old neighborhood. The building has three floors, where people with disabilities live individually in their own apartments. At that time, I was 38 years old.

The new apartment looked nice and clean. There was a black sofa with three seats and a smaller sofa across from it with a table in between. Behind the big sofa were two windows with white curtains and shades. The table had space for my textbooks and notebooks. To the left there was a computer desk. To the right, a television. The place already felt like home.

The living room and kitchen were studio styled, one big room spread into two sections. The bedroom had a closet with two doors. Next to the bed there was a night table with a small lamp. The bathroom was big enough for a wheelchair. When all my belongings were in the new apartment, I was called to sign the last papers. I had lost track of all the papers that I had signed during the previous months.

Moving into the new apartment on my own without Mami and Papi at my side, was a major challenge for me. I was full of joy and courage, but I also felt anxiety. I was uncertain about what lay ahead. I wasn't sure if making the choice to live on my own was the right decision. Everything surrounding me was new: A new way of life, new faces, new place to live, and a whole new environment. It was similar to the change I went through when I first moved from the

DR to Paterson. Except this time, I moved to a place within only minutes from my old neighborhood. And my parents were not there with me.

Fortunately my brother was by my side, helping me to carry my personal belongings and offering his support, which was fundamental during the transition from living with my parents to living thousands of miles away from them. After everything was moved in, Alfredo and I had lunch together. He seemed happy and relieved to see me finally moving to my own spot. He was also impressed by how clean and organized the apartment looked. That made me feel better.

When I returned to my apartment after lunch, one of the staff members, Isaura, who called herself Izzy, helped me unpack. An advantage of this apartment building was that staff was always available to assist the residents. Izzy was a nice young lady, who worked mainly on weekends and occasionally on weekdays, like the day I moved in. She was the building's only Hispanic staff member, so it was helpful to have a Spanish-speaking person to assist me.

We put away my clothes, photo albums, and books. I brought my own dinner plate and a bowl from home to stay connected with my past. We also set up the computer that Papi bought me after I graduated from PCCC. Izzy was a great help in all of this.

My next task was to make a grocery list to go shopping. Izzy helped me because I was unsure what to include in the list. We would be going shopping that evening, but then I would not have a chance to shop again until for another two weeks, according to the residence schedule. I didn't know what items to include besides the basics such as milk, bread, eggs, coffee, and water. Fortunately, Izzy helped me to create the list by suggesting other items that I might need such as salt, sugar, oil, and white rice.

That evening Izzy took me to Shop-Rite. Once we arrived, she grabbed a shopping cart and my shopping list. We headed upstairs as Izzy studied the list. Pushing the cart through the aisles, she grabbed items from the shelves and put them into the cart.

In the past, I rarely went to the market with Mami. Now, here I was with an unfamiliar person in an unfamiliar place, and it all felt wild to me. I had a gift card of $100 to spend, and I was concerned about overspending or choosing the wrong items. Since Izzy was an experienced shopper, she took charge.

At the end of the trip, it was clear that she did very well. We spent the exact amount of money on my card. Over time, Izzy and I became friends and shopped together regularly. About a year after I moved in, Izzy got a new job and moved on. Since then, I sometimes went food shopping with another staff member, but most often, I went with my brother. Food shopping, which once seemed so challenging, had become a normal part of my life

Keeping House

Now, in addition to my school work, I had complete responsibility for my household. I had to do laundry, cook, wash dishes and keep the apartment neat. Due to the CP, I took extra time to do even the small tasks. There were times when it was overwhelming, and I sometimes felt scared of being unable to keep up with everything.

Even though there were staffers available all the time, I did most tasks on my own for two major reasons. First, the supervised apartment was designed for independent living, meaning I was in charge of taking care of most of my needs. Second, I wanted to be more independent and the only way to accomplish that was by relying less on the staff.

Sometimes after a hard day, the thought of giving up on college and going back to the DR to be with my parents crossed my mind. I could take the easy way out, call my parents, and say "Mami and Papi, buy me an airfare. I am coming back to you. I will leave everything behind. I will forget my dreams of being educated and becoming independent."

But in the morning, when I was rushing to get ready for my ride to college, I asked myself what I really wanted to do with my life. Did I really want to go back to that old life, or did I want to keep working toward my goals, despite the challenges that I was facing? I knew that if I went back, I would be happy at first, because I would be with Mami and Papi. I would not have to worry about household responsibilities or school assignments.

But that would last for a short time, because after a while, I would get bored. I had outgrown that life and would probably ask myself why I went back. One day, this debate in my head was settled. After one of my classes at WPU was over, I realized who I had become. I perceived myself as a powerful individual capable of fighting for my goals. To increase my confidence, I applied a technique that I read about. I focused on recalling the major challenges from my past, and remembering how I had overcome the obstacles.

If I stay in New Jersey and focus on my goals, the outcome could certainly be positive I thought. After all, I had already reached several goals that once seemed impossible for me to achieve. When I thought back to my journalism classes and how the professors talked about the impact that journalists had on people's lives, my desire to write my own story and share it with readers increased.

I often hear people saying knowledge is power, but I didn't know how true that was until I experienced it in my personal life. Obtaining my college degree gave me the feeling of power that I had looked for over the years.

My first apartment

CHAPTER 13

FRIENDSHIP

Friendship was not a part of my youth. During my childhood I had no friends in the DR because people there avoided people with disabilities. Once in a while I played with some of the girls my age from my neighborhood. As we grew older, the friendships changed. Some moved out of town; others hung out with their friends from school.

They were able to do things that I wasn't able to do or that I would do very differently, like taking a walk to the park, a common pastime there. Sometimes, I think I may have created more distance between the other girls and myself by not approaching them, because I was self-conscious about being different physically.

When I came to the US as a teenager and started formal school, I looked forward to having girlfriends who would remain my friends forever, but language was a major barrier in trying to make new friends, because I didn't speak English. It was even hard for me to ask, "What are you doing today after school?" Yet, despite that issue, I was well-accepted by my classmates.

By my second school year, I became friendly with three girls in my class. I spent most of my time with Mily, who was from Puerto Rico and two years older than I. We exchanged phone numbers and called each other once in a while. Over the phone, Mily spoke perfect Spanish. We talked about Spanish soap operas and chatted the way I always hoped I would do with a girlfriend. Sometimes, though, when we were at school with others, Mily would not speak Spanish with me, so I felt left out.

The fact that Mily spoke Spanish and also had a disability gave us a common bond. Even though we initially exchanged friendly words like *hola*, *como estas*, (hi, how are you?), it took me time to see Mily as a friend because of her personality. One day she was in a good mood. The next day she wasn't. I was the type of person who tried to keep some distance between myself and a moody person.

Sometimes that was impossible with Mily, because the teacher would ask her to help me with English, since Mily was bilingual. Ms. Angela gave Mily flashcards with various images, such as cars, people, dogs, etc. and Mily taught me the English translation, just as my speech therapist had done. Having Mily in the role of a tutor brought us closer together, even when she wasn't in a good mood.

As I got to know Mily better, I could tell when she was in a good mood and when she wasn't. Her facial expression said all. We rode the same school bus. In the morning, I was picked up first. The front door of Mily's house had a few steps. Mily's mother would hold her daughter's hand, and with the other hand, she carried Mily's crutches.

Sometimes when Mily got on the bus, she didn't want to talk and socialize. She showed no sign of friendship and would sit two seats ahead of me. Her silence meant that she didn't want to be bothered. So on those days I tried to keep my distance.

In the middle of the school year, there were several days when the school bus didn't pick up Mily. At school, I heard some of the staff talking about a death in her family. A week later, the school bus picked her up, but we didn't talk until that evening, when she called me at home. Her voice sounded sad, but she seemed willing to talk and told me about her father passing away a week before. I felt sorry for her.

Mily graduated a year after I transferred to my new school. In the meantime, we kept calling one another until she moved back to Puerto Rico. Unfortunately we didn't have a chance to say goodbye in person. I did feel sad to find out that she was moving, but sometimes, that's just the way it is. Mily moved from Paterson to Puerto Rico, just as I once moved from the DR to Paterson. It has been many years since Mily moved back to Puerto Rico. We lost contact with each other a long time ago.

Scott

A good friendship can knock down any barrier, even differences in language and culture. Scott and I got along well. We were both students at the CP Center, were the same age and shared birthday months. When we had to work on school projects, we helped one another even though at the beginning. I didn't understand what Scott meant when he said something to me. Sometimes I felt bad because I didn't know how to respond in English, but Scott never gave up on me. Instead of teaching me English, he wanted me to teach him Spanish, so I taught him some basic words. *hola, ¿Como estas?*

We also worked together on school projects and tasks. After lunch, students worked in pairs to do the dishes. Scott and I did this chore twice a week, since our disability was less severe physically compared with our classmates who did the dishes only once a week.

As time passed, our friendship grew. After a while, we exchanged phone numbers, and Scott called me on weekends. Later on, his older sister, Elaine, who majored in special education, did an internship at our school. Sometimes during the summer, she took us out to the movies, or Scott's parents invited me over for barbeques and to go out to restaurants with them. At that time, Scott and I were both 19.

Twenty years have passed since I left school, but Scott and I are still friends. We talk on the phone, send each other Christmas cards, and meet occasionally at events, especially the annual dinner dance hosted each May by Special Olympics of Passaic County. I was involved with Special Olympics in the past and still attend their events.

A year ago, Scott had to go through a major surgery. Weeks before, he called to let me know what was going on and asked me to pray for him. When he was released from the hospital. I called him at home to find out how he was doing and was happy when he recovered well. Though we don't see each other often, Scott and I share a bond made stronger by the fact that we both face the challenges of living life with a disability.

David

I was 16 when I met David at school too, but we were not in the same classroom, because he was a few years younger. We sat together on the school bus and had long conversations. Despite his young age, David was mature and loved talking about current events.

His parents were from Colombia, so even though David was born in New Jersey, he spoke fluent Spanish. His mother was member of the parents' advocacy group, where Mami and I were also members. Sometimes I saw David on Saturdays, when we had special events at the group. David also has CP, so it was easy for us to feel close to each other.

Over the years, David and I became close friends. Many people thought we had a romantic relationship, because we called each other on the phone very often, and whenever he came to the advocacy group, we sat together. People assumed we were dating, but we weren't. We were just good friends.

David and I don't see each as often as we used to. We do keep in touch through phone calls, text messages, and Facebook. David is the kind of person who likes to help others. He volunteers at a local day program for adults with disabilities. Due to their physical disabilities, some of them find it very challenging to use modern technology, so David assists them with that.

He also helps to support a musical band, Atril, from Colombia. The musicians are blind and often lack resources to buy instruments or travel for concerts and interviews. David met Atril 15 years ago during a visit to Colombia and was very moved by their lack of support. Once he returned from the trip, David set out to find a sponsor for the band, but unfortunately, he has not been able to do so. In the meantime, he continues to find other ways to help them.

With the support of his mother and some friends, David sells chocolate bars, bottles of water, and Atril's music CDs. The money they raise helps Atril meet expenses.

David has tried to get a regular job, but due to his physical disability, he has not succeeded. After graduating from high school, he looked for a job and at one point, was close to getting hired. However, once the employer found out that David had physical challenge the position was denied. He has made other attempts to find employment without success.

It is unfortunate that someone who is so caring, willing to work hard, and successful at fundraising has been overlooked by employers because of a disability that does not affect all his talents. Meantime David continues to use those talents by volunteering, helping the band, and remaining active in his church.

CHAPTER 14

FIRST ROMANCE

Back in 1997, I saw Persio each week at the parents' group advocacy meetings. As time passed, a special bond developed between us. He was still a shy and quiet young man. I tried my best to encourage him to move ahead in life. He was in his early 20s, yet he had a hard time dealing with the transition from the teen years to adulthood.

Even though I was struggling in college at the time, I tried to support Persio by helping him to develop his full potential as a person. I knew that he was capable. He just needed to hear somebody say, "You can do it." I knew how important that was, since people supported me with words like that. Probably nobody had said that to Persio before, which was a real shame.

Persio knew a lot about music and played a couple of instruments. Whenever I was listening to a song and wanted to learn more about it, I just had to call Persio and ask him. He always knew the right answers about music. I was aware of his talent and his high intelligence, so I didn't want to leave him behind while I was working hard to accomplish my own goals.

Persio tried several times to earn a college degree and actually attended PCCC, too, but he dropped out after a short while. He wanted to get into the music industry as a music engineer. We lived close to New York City which was a great market when it came to music, so Persio tried to find information about resources available there. After a while, though, he wasn't convinced this would work out for him, because he would have to commute to New York, and didn't feel he could do that with his visual impairment.

Persio had kept me posted regarding all the steps that he was taking to get into music. While pursuing my own dream, I enjoyed supporting his, too. Together we investigated local colleges that had music programs, and we visited Montclair State University and Bergen Community College (BCC). Persio liked them, and applied to both. He enrolled at BCCC where he did well during the first semester, but dropped out the next semester.

I realized Persio's problem was bigger than I had imagined, and it took me time to become aware of the issue. At home he lacked support, which is fundamental to move ahead. In my case I had the courage to fight for my goals, because I had support from my family, especially from my mother.

His glaucoma was the excuse that Persio's mother used to prevent him from growing as a person. She made Persio believe that if he enrolled again in college or in a music program, his eyesight would be affected, because he would rely too much on his eyes. She never encouraged him to explore the alternatives that existed for people who are blind or visually impaired,

When Persio was in high school, he used a device that helped him to read better. It looked like a computer monitor. He placed the book under the monitor and adjusted the font to suit his eyes. The device was placed on a transportable table with four small wheels. Whenever I was in class and I heard the sound of the wheels. I knew Persio was on his way to the classroom.

After his failed college attempts, he had been accepted into a program run by the Commission for the Blind and Visually Impaired to help clients become more independent and productive. Persio learned to use Braille, which is a helpful skill and may even become necessary for him, since people with glaucoma are at risk of losing their sight as they age. Yet he was still unable to move forward.

Through it all, Persio and I enjoyed being with each other. On weekends we visited each other. We even spent Thanksgiving, Christmas, and Easter together, rotating the holidays between our families. If Persio came to my house on Christmas Eve, I would spend Christmas Day at his house, or vice versa.

We were each becoming part of the other's family, sharing dinners and birthday parties together. Often our family members would drive us when we wanted to go somewhere. If there was something special going on in my family, like a barbeque in the summer, and Persio wasn't there, my relatives asked for him. We even shared in family reunions.

My relatives treated Persio nicely, and I always felt welcomed by his family, but I was still introduced just as a friend, not as his girlfriend. I didn't think of Persio as just a friend anymore. I wanted more from him.

His older sister Miguelina sometimes invited us to go out with her, and seemed to realize we were more than just friends. She invited my parents and me to her wedding, and at the reception, she came to our table and with a sweet smile said, "You guys will be next." I hoped she was right.

It was only after a few years of knowing each other and doing things together, we had our first real date alone together. It was a sunny and hot Saturday afternoon. Persio scheduled a ride with Access Link, the transportation service he had introduced to me. We were picked up at my house and dropped off outside the Willowbrook Mall, a major shopping center. As we walked through the entrance near the food court, we held hands. It was a great experience, to be going out together as a couple, just the two of us.

Before then, every time we went out, somebody came with us. This time, we had a feeling of freedom. We stopped first at the food court, ordered some Taco Bell, and sat at a nearby table. As we ate together, we laughed and talked, adding our voices to all the other lively conservations around us.

After lunch, Persio and I walked around, looking in shop windows and visiting some stores. When it was time to go, we went outside and sat on a bench to wait for our ride home. It had been a happy day for both of us.

Persio was a romantic. Every Valentine's Day he came to my house even if it was snowing outside. To him, it was very important that we spend Valentine's Day together. He brought me a card, a box of chocolates, and two big balloons with a heart and the words "I Love You." In the card was a message: *"I love you ma. From your pa Persio!"* We called each other by nicknames. It was our special way of communicating and made our relationship closer. I called him pa and he called me ma.

Persio and I had good communication and mutual respect. I appreciated that he supported the priority I placed on my academic responsibilities, especially if that meant I was too busy for one of our regular phone chats. We talked about everything that mattered to us, big and small. We talked about what we did early that day, about our families, and about ourselves as individuals and as a couple.

I was the first one to bring up the subject of spending our lives together. Traditionally men are the ones who start this type of conversation, but I decided to take the initiative after he kissed me one evening. It was our first kiss and took me by surprise. Persio and I were sitting next to each other.

His arms were around my shoulders. Suddenly he turned his face toward me and kissed me. That first kiss was like unexpectedly finding a buried treasure I had been hunting for without knowing where it was hidden. The kiss gave me the courage to bring up the subject of marriage.

Soon, Persio and I started researching housing assistance for couples with disabilities and made an appointment with my former case manager. Michael explained that there was a problem, since Persio wasn't registered with the agency we consulted about assistance. He suggested that Persio contact the Commission for the Blind and Visually Impaired for help. The idea was to have both agencies work together and come up with a plan that would assist us financially.

This happened in the spring of 2007, when I was still going to PCCC and also getting professional help for my depression. Persio was a great support to me during this stressful time. Whenever I was feeling sad or sick I told him. He called every day to check on me. Then one day, I told him what happened to me earlier, when suicidal thoughts entered my mind.

"I am telling you this just in case something happens to me," I said. He was the only person I ever told about that. Persio responded in a sweet tone of voice, "Don't worry, ma. Nothing bad will happen to you." I felt comforted. "Thank you, pa," I told him. "I love you."

Since neither of us had ever been married, we thought it would be a good idea to see a marriage counselor before we took the step. We decided to see my godfather, Dr. Lugo, who is a marriage counselor as well as a high school teacher. Persio had been in his class, too, and knew Dr. Lugo, so I suggested he call and make the counseling appointment. I could have done it, but I wanted Persio to take charge of this, so he could have a sense of power and manhood.

We brought a basket of fruit as a token of appreciation for Dr. Lugo taking time out of his busy schedule to talk to us. We told him our concerns regarding sexuality and other matters that we would face in a marriage. After the session was over, I felt pleased. I thought the talk would help Persio and me in our relationship.

The Real Test

Mami always told me her opinion, regardless of how painful it could be for me. One day at lunch time, Mami initiated an important conversation, by pointing out Persio's positive qualities. "He is a nice muchacho," she said. But then, she said the words I expected, but didn't want to hear. *"Ahy, mi'hija yo lo veo muy flojo."* She told me Persio didn't have the guts it takes as a man to be married. She wasn't the first person to express that opinion to me, but I was in denial.

Persio didn't have an active life. Back then, I thought that could be changed and that I could help him to make the change. He would spend most of the day at home, helping his mother around the house. It took me a while to realize that his situation needed special attention.

I encouraged him to seek professional help. I realized that low self-esteem was the major cause of the problem, since his mother didn't build a feeling of confidence in him. She was overprotective and made him feel insecure about taking the next step in his career choices and relationships. Persio listened to my suggestion and decided to go for counseling.

He talked to me about the counseling sessions with his psychologist and seemed very positive. To me his reaction was a good sign and showed improvement. Persio continued to see the psychologist over the next few months. I was stupid in love, and to me it seemed everything was going well.

All during that time, I was going through my own depression and was seeing a psychologist, too. In fact, I was seeing the same psychologist as Persio. At first, I wasn't sure if that was a good idea, but in my culture it is common to obtain references from a relative or a friend, instead of from another expert. When I had difficulty finding a counselor, Persio suggested his, but we attended our counseling sessions individually and never met at the clinic. Our conversations with the counselor remained confidential.

The Breakup

Some time had passed and I again brought up the subject of marriage. For the first time in our years together, I had to ask Persio to be honest with me, because this was a major step. It was late summer 2007. On a Sunday evening he came to my house. We sat together at the computer where I created a new file called "Wedding List." Then we started to make concrete plans for the wedding. We set the date for summer 2008, but I never imagined what was about to happen.

A couple of days later, Persio called me to tell me over the phone that we would not be getting married. The news stunned me, but I needed to hear him say what we had to say in person. I let him know that a phone call was not the appropriate way to tell me this news. I thought his behavior was immature, and I asked Persio to meet in person. His excuse didn't make sense to me. I thought he was afraid of getting married.

The next day, he came to my house. No one else was at home, so we had privacy to talk. We went upstairs to the same room where we had started our wedding list He got down on his knees and started to cry like a baby, asking me to forgive him. I didn't know how to react. I was upset about the turn of events, but at the same time, it broke my heart to see him cry. I looked at him and said, "Persio, please get up. Stop crying." Then I asked him to leave. I was so upset about the way he was acting that I didn't want to talk.

Persio went downstairs to wait for his ride home, and I followed him. It was a warm day so he sat to wait on the doorstep. I sat two steps up. I didn't want to leave him by himself. Though I was hurt by what happened, I felt compassion, since it was obvious that he was devastated. While waiting, we didn't talk. When his ride arrived, Persio grabbed the cane he sometimes used and walked toward the bus.

He took a couple of steps and stopped. He turned to look at me and, holding the cane in his right hand, waved to me with his left hand. In a sad tone of voice he said goodbye. I was so upset that I was unable to cry. I thought Mami was right. Persio didn't have the guts to save our relationship.

When Mami returned home from her job, I told her what had happened. Mami said she didn't feel too sorry for me, because I would move on. She did feel deeply sorry for Persio, though, because of his lack of determination.

Going through a break-up after years of being together was hard for me. Even though I was the one who decided to end our relationship, I still hoped that we would get back together. Actually, I did not so much break-up as give us a time out. I suggested Persio take some time to think about our future together and we set a date when we would talk again. During that period we seldom called each other.

Despite Persio's confusion, I still wanted to give him a chance to decide, because I knew his love was real. I knew for sure that he loved me and that even when I was going through tough times, I always could count on him. His big heart and the way we treated each other made me feel that he was the man that I wanted to spend the rest of my life with.

When the time out ended, Persio had decided that we would not get back together. Of course I felt sad, because I still hoped he could change, but at the same time I tried to be strong. I didn't let that breakup take control over my life.

More than seven years have passed, since then. Once in a while Persio and I have encountered each other at the programs we attend for people with disabilities. When I see him, my heart breaks thinking how different our lives could have been and how miserable a life he must be living, not pursuing his dreams.

Last summer, we met again at a barbecue. I approached him and asked what he was up to. I really felt sorry for Persio, because he was 37, but his life had not changed since the day we parted. It broke my heart to see the sadness in his face.

Persio is a wonderful person with a big heart who needed someone to guide him. I tried my best to be that person for him, so he could have a better quality of life and so we could spend the rest of our lives together. I was disappointed that things didn't work out, but looking back, that may have been better for me. I have been able to move on and accomplish my goals. I now understand why Mami didn't feel as sorry for me as she felt for Persio.

CHAPTER 15

GRADUATION DAY: I MADE IT.

On May 15, 2013 I reached another major goal. I earned my bachelor of arts degree in communication with a concentration in print journalism and a minor in English. The ceremony was held at the Izod Center, a large arena in East Rutherford, New Jersey. My parents, Alfredo, Soris, and my friend David were all there to see me receive my diploma.

As I sat, in my cap and gown, waiting to be called to go up onstage to receive my diploma, I could hardly believe it was really happening. I felt like the main character of a fairy tale where the happy ending goes beyond the expectations of the readers.

I was about to receive my bachelor's degree from William Paterson University. The diploma I was about to receive symbolized so much: My hard work in school; my ability to overcome the obstacles of my physical limitations and language barrier; my success at reaching my goals. My diploma proved how important it was to follow my dreams and fight very hard to achieve them.

The diploma I would hold in my hands was the result of courage, sleep deprivation, perseverance, and determination. It was the evidence I needed to prove that I could do it.

Most important, it symbolized that the support I received from my family and the strength I got from God were more powerful than the limitations society tried to impose on me.

Everybody at the ceremony was thrilled to hear my name called and to see me walking up to the stage, with a staff member holding my left arm, to receive my diploma. Mami was holding her camera trying to take the best shots, since she and Papi were closer to the stage. After the ceremony was over and the rest of the graduates went to meet with their families and friends, Mami walked toward where I was sitting and took more photos.

Then my parents and I joined Alfredo, Soris, and David who were waiting in their seats. From there we went to a Cuban restaurant for lunch. When we returned home, I received phone calls, e-mail messages, and gifts from relatives and friends who had supported me in my efforts to reach this goal and wanted to congratulate me. It was a wonderful day. I made it.

Once again, my story made the daily newspapers. *The Record* and *The Herald News* published an article about a few of the graduates, and I was one of them. The article briefly covered some of the major events in my life as a student and described my future plans. I described my plans for the non-profit, but not the memoir. I didn't want to make it public yet.

After Graduation

After graduation. I continued working on the memoir. Finishing the book became my major goal. Since Professor

Hillringhouse introduced me to the art of expressing myself through writing, I had come to see the publication of books as something fascinating. I couldn't wait to see my name in print on the front cover of a book.

When my final semester at WPU was over, Dr. Lesher continued to help me with the editing task. Soon I realized that writing a memoir and getting it ready to submit to a publisher wasn't as easy as I had thought, especially for a first-time book author. I had to work and wait, over and over

I also learned I couldn't do it all alone. A manuscript needs to go through several stages. My writing it and the second person editing weren't enough. I needed at least two people who were good readers to review the manuscript and provide feedback. Most of the people I knew didn't have strong reading skills. Those who did have the skills also had a tight schedule. After asking several potential readers, I finally found the right people.

It was early November 2014 and I was still living in the supervised apartment, the same place that I was living before my graduation in May 2013. By then some of my relatives and acquaintances asked me what I had being doing since graduation. "Are you working? Are you looking for a job?" The excuse that I used for not working was the nationwide recession. "You know, nowadays it is hard to find a job because of the current economy," I would say. I don't think everybody believed me, but at least I evaded further discussion.

Having a college degree should have been the tool I needed to move ahead. This meant working at a job with a decent pay and supporting myself financially. At this point, that was not the case, since my social and economic status was still the same. But some believed I should have moved on to a different stage in my life and I had to admit, they had good reasons to think so. I now had a college degree and am also bilingual. Not everybody has these advantages.

Employment

My goals at the time were to run my own non-profit and keep working on my memoir. Since the non-profit was already registered, the next step was to get in partnership with other non-profits that had similar objectives. I reached out to a couple of organizations to see if I could get the support needed to get started. Unfortunately, that did not work out.

As a result, I decided to put aside the idea of running Rainbow Of Talent for a while and focus on my memoir. Some people thought that trying to get a regular job in my field would have been the logical thing to do, but I had my mind set on those two goals.

I realized that I couldn't work on both projects at the same time, since both are time consuming. Holding down a job while doing either of them was also too much. Plus, I had household responsibilities like doing laundry, cooking, trying to keep the apartment as neat as possible, and taking care of my personal needs. Those were rough tasks for a person with physical challenges and I had to consider that overdoing things could lead to serious medical issues for me. So I made the decision to focus first on my memoir.

Fortunately, a large part of my expenses for housing, utilities, food, and other necessities were being covered by my Social Security income and allowances from social service agencies. This took care of electricity bills, phone, cable, and part of the rent. I did pay my own cell phone bills. I could have gotten a free phone, but it would not provide long distance calls and I wanted to keep connected to my parents in the DR.

Though I had financial assistance, I realized I was no longer living with my parents and had to manage my own money and spend it wisely. Every month I had to send certain amount of money to DDD, one of the agencies helping me. This money was called "contribution to care." This meant that since the state was covering most of my daily expenses I had the responsibility to help with the cost. I sent whatever I could afford.

When I was still attending college and Alfredo couldn't take me to school, I had to take Access Link which provided transportation for people with disabilities at reduced price. I also had to buy lunch at school and meet other routine expenses. Plus, I had a student loan facing me.

Months after I graduated from WPU, it was time to start paying off the loan. Since I was not working, I wasn't able to make the monthly $400 payment. On the other hand, I didn't want to skip the payment which could create bad credit. I went online to the federal student loan web page to see what options they had for college graduates who were unable to keep up with monthly payments. I learned about the Pay as You Earn Plan, which meant payment amounts would be based on income. I filled out the application form and mailed it with a copy of my SSI award letter, which stated my proof of annual income.

Having my expenses covered that way wasn't as much fun as some people might think. In fact, a few people asked me why I should worry about getting a job if every month I receive a check from SSI and a place to live. Yes, to certain point there was a logic to what they said, but I felt they were making a judgment. I didn't respond back.

However, I told myself I wanted to earn my own money when I am capable of doing it. This is not just about having my basic needs met. It is about feeling worthier as a person. It is about being able to contribute to my community. It is about being active. It is about being financially independent. It is about having the power to make any choice that I want with the money that I earn, not with the money that taxpayers pay.

Both of my parents worked, and I had learned from them that one of the greatest satisfactions that a person can experience is working hard with the *sudor de su frente*, (sweat of his brow), and being able to spend the money that was earned decently. So that's want I want to do. From personal experience, I know that acquiring material possessions without working hard to earn them, can lead to taking things for granted. That is not what I want to spend the rest of my life doing.

CHAPTER 16

THERAPEUTIC WRITING AND A CARING MENTOR GAVE MY LIFE NEW MEANING

Back in 2002 when I returned to PCCC, I didn't know what I wanted in life. I was like a driver driving a car without a clear destination. Though I returned to college, I felt lost. I lost faith in people, in life and even in myself. All I knew was that I wanted to obtain a college degree.

But then, I found my meaning and purpose when I met Professor Hillringhouse who helped me to realize I am a writer. He encouraged me and challenged me, first with those goofy poems, then with the translation exercises. Finally, he motivated me to look inside myself and start writing from within.

I wrote about the happy memories from my childhood in the DR, the games I used to play with my brothers, the first time I saw snow, my first dinner in Paterson with my family, and being re-united with my father after four years. Moments that had a big impact on me.

Sharing happy moments through writing was easy and fun. But then, Professor Hillringhouse pushed me to dig deeper and write about the tough things in my life: sadness, frustration, anger, failures, discrimination. To be able to express those hard emotions and experiences requires patience, time, courage, motivation and, in my case, inspiration from someone who has already done that.

When Professor Hillringhouse first suggested I write about a painful time in my life, I thought he was being cruel to me. I didn't want to relive unhappy times or reveal the hurtful things that happened to me. Then one evening I decided to read some of the poems the professor wrote. He had given them to me weeks earlier, but I didn't read them right away.

When I finally did, I was completely stunned by his poem Route 80 and by the idea of a man expressing his feelings that way. I didn't realize yet how therapeutic it could be to write about your pain. I had been trying to avoid that.

Writing about myself helped me to become aware of the wounds I had carried with me all my life. They were not visible, but kept hidden within my unconscious and my soul. They were very difficult to heal because nobody could see them. I wasn't aware of how much the wounds were affecting me until I wrote about them.

I wanted to keep them in secret for a couple of reasons. First, my self-esteem was low. I felt insecure about people and about myself. I had been discouraged by a number of people at different stages of my life, and the effects of their negative criticisms were still within me. Second, going through all those evaluations that mostly highlighted my weaknesses caused me to distrust others, sometimes even Professor Hillringhouse. When he first seemed impressed with my writing, I wasn't sure if he meant it, or just tried to make me feel better.

Reading his poems helped me to start opening myself up. Also, the support that I received when Professor Hillringhouse said "Juana, you are getting there. Keep up the good work," made a difference, because it meant that I was making progress even if just a little at a time. The results of therapeutic writing didn't happen overnight. That process took time.

At home, I sat in front of the computer, went back in time, and started typing. All those emotions that I had not revealed came to the surface, and I had the courage to let them all out. I was following my mentor's instructions by describing a situation and then explaining how I felt about it at that time.

I wrote about my experiences as an immigrant, spending four years without seeing my father, living with CP, and lacking formal education. The most painful was to write about my physical appearance and the way I had been teased by other children, excluded from so many things, and pitied by strangers. I described how disconnected I felt from Papi when I first moved from the DR, and how devastated I was by my Abuelo's death. Moving to a new country…attending school for the first time…making friends. I wrote about all those things.

Some experiences I had never revealed to anyone until I started creating poems. It was much easier to express certain parts of myself through poetry. This was the moment when writing became a form of therapy to start healing my turmoil from the past, even from the turmoil of writing itself.

I realized the big difference between academic and therapeutic writing. One was about the pressure to follow rules and get good grades. The other was a way to release my feelings, emotions, and thoughts. Every time I practiced therapeutic writing, I experienced a sensation of freedom as never before I had felt.

With Professor Hillringhouse telling me "Good job, Juana," I gained confidence as a writer. Many of my haiku translations were published in my uncle's magazine *Mi Revista*, a monthly publication in the DR. I also wrote articles in Spanish for the magazine. One day I made the front page when I wrote an article about living in the DR with CP. This was a major event for me as a writer and for the publication, because people with disabilities often don't make the front page of a publication, especially in the DR.

Summer was the time when I focused on the therapeutic writing. Throughout the academic year, I didn't have much time to devote to personal writing. Professor Hillringhouse didn't want me to neglect my academic responsibilities. He was on top of me literally all the time motivating me to study hard.

During the summer, I met with Prof Hillringhouse once a week around 2:00 pm, after he was done with taking care if his job responsibilities. By then, he had been promoted to the position of distance learning specialist. Together, we reviewed my weekly writing and reading work. There were times when I wrote 40 haiku per week. That was a lot.

A big part of our communication took place through e-mails. When I had a question about the writing or the assignments I sent Professor Hillringhouse an e-mail. When he had time, he responded. Throughout the week I wrote new drafts of essays and poetry and also spent time reading. Even though I wasn't taking any course officially, I was very active with the mentoring. There was no pressure about my work being graded, so it was enjoyable, yet still important.

As a writer, I learned the lessons of professionalism from Professor Hillringhouse. When we were working on a project, he stressed the quality of the work, not just getting it done by a certain due date. Also he made sure that I learned from these projects. If there was something that I didn't understand, the professor worked with me until I grasped it.

There were occasions when I arrived at his office and he had not had chance to eat lunch, because he was taking care his of job duties in order to have time for our mentoring session. I was impressed by such dedication.

Before I came to know Professor Hillringhouse, when I was in a classroom and I saw a professor giving a lecture, I saw that professor as someone perfect, someone who does not have major problems. But from knowing and working with Professor Hillringhouse, I realized that my professors were people with their own struggles and issues who still managed to do good and be creative.

In the fall semester of 2006, I had to drop my environmental science course, because I wasn't passing the tests. I was feeling bad, because I couldn't keep up with two courses at the same time. After I dropped, I stopped by Professor Hillringhouse's office. He noticed that I was feeling sad and seemed to sense the reason.

He looked straight into my eyes and said "I know how you are feeling." Then he grabbed his wallet, and took out an ID card and showed it to me. "I am a student too," he said. I was surprised hearing that my professor was a student too. He had returned to school for his Master of Fine Arts degree. That taught me that learning is a lifelong process.

While he was teaching full-time at PCCC and going to school for his MFA, Professor Hillringhouse was going through the most difficult time in his life. He had to cope with his father's illness and death. Then, his mother suffered a stroke and was later involved in s car accident, making it impossible for her to take care for herself. Professor Hillringhouse became his mother's caregiver for five years until she passed away.

Through all of that, he continued to mentor me. During one of the mentoring sessions, I asked him why he was helping me. He responded, "Because we are here to help one another." What a beautiful concept, I thought.

To this day, we remain in touch, and recently, I asked him that same question again, "Despite everything, you were always there for me," I said. "Offering your support, encouraging me to keep on while you were dealing with your own suffering. Why?" I recalled that he once said he liked my poems and my spirit and asked him why he did. This is how he responded:

"I liked your spirit because you never appeared sad or mad at what you had to go through and you were always beaming with a smile which made me feel good and humbled me. If you could smile through what you were going through, then who was I to complain? That was the gift of your spirit. Your poems had the same spirit in them. That is why I liked them so much."

I was very touched by that response. We were both going through a tough time in our lives, and despite all the obstacles that I was going through. I tried to keep smiling. I thought that being upset didn't help my situation. I have big teeth and most of the time, my mouth is partly open, probably due to the CP. I never saw anything special in my smile, but it has always attracted attention from others. People often tell me I have a nice smile. Once, someone told me a long time ago, "Don't let anyone prevent you from smiling."

Since I have a few risk factors that can contribute to the decline of my physical health - the CP, my age, and my gender - it is important for me to remain physically active, so I go regularly for physical therapy. One of the other clients at the therapy facility, a sweet lady named Virginia told me recently, "What a nice smile. I love your smile."

So I keep smiling, even when going through difficult times in my life. Sometimes, when I arrived at Professor Hillringhouse's office, he looked sad, probably due to his personal situation at the time. In his poem, "Orpheus" he writes about that stage of his life:

> *"My worst fear was being stuck*
> *after dad died, and then her stroke,*
> *the car accident, taking care of her*
> *For five years until she gave up*
> *and I gave so little."*

Our poetry was becoming more than symbolic language crafted with metaphors, imagery, and stanzas. It was becoming a link that bonded the two of us, student and professor, from very different backgrounds. I was just a young adult, a person with disability, a Latina and a female who was trying to break down many barriers at once by pursuing my ambitious dream of earning a college degree.

From my mentor, I learned one of biggest lessons in my life. Regardless of our differences, every one of us can touch another life with an act of kindness, a smile, or with some words of encouragement like "You are getting there."

CHAPTER 17

A REFLECTION ABOUT MY JOURNEY

I see myself as much more than the person with cerebral palsy. I do not let my disability define me. My soul and my intellectual abilities are stronger than my physical body. For many years I was caught up in what I was unable to do physically. I never paid attention to my intellectual abilities and my spirituality.

To make matters worse, for many years, I dwelled on reasons why I have this body. I knew the medical explanation for my CP was lack of oxygen in my brain at the time of birth. But I wondered why that happened to me? Now I am able to say that God had created me with a purpose. Thanks to the gift of writing that God has given me, I have found my purpose in life.

Looking back at my life I can say that I have come far, but I realize I haven't made it by myself. I feel thankful that my accomplishments were made possible with the support that I had received from others: Mami, Papi, my family, my godfather, kind professors, dedicated counselors, and other caring people who appeared in my life with both friendship and assistance.

At one time, achieving a high school education seemed like an unbelievable dream. Yet, today, I am a college graduate with a bachelor's degree. I have become more independent, learned to live on my own, and even fell in love. All this makes me feel proud of myself.

I have achieved a level of maturity most people didn't think possible for a person with my disability. I am even open to falling in love again, but I don't let that thought run my life. If romance comes again, it will be welcome. If not, I can still move on. In the meantime, I look forward to the publication of my first book, I hope it will be the first of many, I also hope it will give inspiration to readers with disabilities of any type. I made it. You can, too.

Special thanks to Professor Mark Hillringhouse, Dr. Christine Redman-Waldeyer and Linda Telesco, all of Passaic County Community College, for their support of this book project. Thanks also to Dr. Tina Lesher of William Paterson University for encouraging this project, since the first day that I announced in her class my dream of writing a memoir.

Last but not least, thanks to the Division of Developmental Disabilities (DDD) for providing housing and financial assistance, so I could focus on my education.

Me and my smile

Getting closer to Papi

Printed in the United States
By Bookmasters